Signalling

Nigel Digby

Ian Allan
PUBLISHING

First published 2010

ISBN 978 0 7110 3427 3

© Nigel Digby 2010

Published by Ian Allan Publishing

an imprint of Ian Allan Publishing Ltd, Hersham, Surrey KT12 4RG.
Printed in England by Ian Allan Printing Ltd, Hersham, Surrey KT12 4RG.

Visit the Ian Allan Publishing website at www.ianallanpublishing.com

Distributed in the United States of America and Canada by
BookMasters Distribution Services.

Code 1010/B2

Title page: *This impressive signal was a product of the Melton Constable concrete shop in 1921,
and was one of a pair of concrete bracket signals at Melton West Junction, the signalbox
bearing that name being visible in the middle distance. As well as being a thing of beauty in
itself, it serves to illustrate several subject areas that are explained in this book. The topmost
stop arm on the centre post is the Down Home for the platform road, and the other Stop arm on
the left-hand 'doll' is the Home for the goods loop. The two arms with fishtails are the splitting
Distant signals for Melton Constable East Junction, out of sight beyond the bridge. The 'slots'
for these signals are the top sets of balance weights at the foot of the post. The hammerhead-
shaped signal on the lower left is a 'Calling-on' arm.* M&GN Archive Trust, courtesy of Ray Meek

Contents

Preface and acknowledgements

You are at the lever frame in your signalbox. Both main platforms of your station are occupied by passenger trains, a goods train is setting back into the yard, and your Down block bell is ringing shrilly with the four beats demanding permission for an express to approach. Should you accept the express with the warning arrangement? Have you got time to dispatch one of the local trains up the branch? Under your collar your neck is feeling distinctly hot. You reach for the bell plunger on your block instrument, sensing the eyes of the District Inspector watching all you are doing.

Then a pleasant lady appears at the door with mugs of railway-strength tea and you are once more in a small room in a suburban house in North Wootton, at the controls of 'Lutton', an O-gauge LMS layout, and the District Inspector dwindles into an amused Frank Roomes, builder of the railway and ex-Royal Engineers Signalling Instructor.

Achieving this illusion is surely one of the aims of our hobby, that participating in the operation of a miniature railway transports you from the real world into the modelled world. The object before you is no longer just a construct of wood, cardboard, plastic and metal, but a living thing, an embodiment of past times in which you can immerse yourself.

The effect on me of the first of many visits to Lutton was profound. All my past efforts seemed dull and lacklustre by comparison. I realised that what had been missing was an entire department of railway life. I resolved that, henceforth, signalling and proper signalbox working would be a cornerstone of my railway modelling.

My thanks on the photographic front must go to Mick Nicholson, Mike Back, Tony Wright (*British Railway Modelling*), John Hobden, Ray Meek and Adrian Whittaker (M&GN Circle). On the editorial front thanks are due to Mick Nicholson, Roger Kingstone and Bob Essery, who added their corrections, suggestions and encouragement, and Peter Waller at Ian Allan. Finally, of course, to Angela, whose support made it possible to write this book, which is dedicated to the memory of the late Frank Roomes.

Nigel Digby
Cromer 2010

Introduction

Signals in the landscape 1: The junction signals at Harecastle on the ex-North Staffordshire Railway were photographed just before Harecastle Tunnel behind them was opened out into a cutting. The LMS enamelled upper-quadrant arms, mounted on the original NSR posts, protect the main line to Macclesfield on the left, and the lesser-status line to Crewe on the right. The track circuit diamond has been mounted on a patch of black paint to give it more contrast.
Ian Allan Library

Signalling is an aspect of the railway scene that fails to receive the attention it deserves. To be fair, the modeller is left very much in the dark concerning this important subject, particularly the younger modeller. There are huge ranges of locomotives, rolling stock and track available for use straight out of the box, but very few useful signals and virtually no guidance about where to put them. That is the purpose of this book, which will indicate the likely position and types of signals, and the typical signalbox-to-signalbox communication that occurred to make the railway safe. This is not to be pedantic, but is solely in order that these aspects can be incorporated in the proper way on a layout set between 1890 and the present day, so that it will look right as well as be operationally correct.

Why use signalling?

Modellers may be excused for asking why they should go to the trouble of learning about signalling. After all, collisions on layouts are usually unlikely due to the constraints of the electrical system, and points are often changed by the operator electrically from a control panel, so why is signalling necessary at all?

It must be appreciated that the signals are as much a part of the modelled environment as the locomotives, buildings or scenery. The whole idea is to recreate an entire slice of history, whether that history be 100 years ago or last week. If you go to the trouble of placing sheep and cows in model fields, then to complete the scene signals certainly must be included. The aim for modellers should be to place the layout in space and time without the aid of a single train being present, and signalling can help them do that. Signals and signalboxes were

Signals in the landscape 2: The pioneering 'Pendon Vale' model, set in about 1930, has taken railway modelling to new peaks of excellence. The signals here assume their rightful place in the overall modelled environment and without them this scene would be incomplete. The small signal with the pair of holes in the arm is a GWR 'Backing' signal. Other vital details such as the point rodding and barrow crossing are also noticeable. Tony Wright, courtesy of British Railway Modelling

not uniform, their designs often being unique to one railway company, and changing over time. By using clues like this, modellers can underpin their layouts with the solid base of history, of 'believability' if you like.

However, it would be a mistake to think of the signals as merely part of the scenery. A common state of affairs on private layouts and some of those on the exhibition circuit is that signals of approximately correct type have been provided but they do not work. Often this is intended to be a temporary state, which extends into a permanent one. Making them function does mean extra work, but having made one aspect of the railway (the locos and rolling stock) as working models, it would be negligent not to do the same for the system that tells the trains when and where to go. Also, apart from the objectionable sight of trains running past signals at Danger, I would point out the increasing number of DCC systems, with no conventional electrical sections and with electronic recognition mounted in each locomotive, allowing simultaneous motion of several at a time. Without some kind of working signalling directing the operators, disaster or at least embarrassment is inevitable.

In short, what I am recommending is the bringing together of point and signal control into a proper working signalbox, with a signalman (or woman) controlling the movement of trains, and communicating with the rest of the model in the correct manner. The difference this makes to the realism and enjoyment of even the simplest layout has to be experienced to be believed. If you do not yet have working signalling, try to visit a model that has.

Planning options

Before venturing into the area of signalling, it would be as well to have a brief look at the whole subject of planning the railway, as the formation of the track and the signals protecting it are inextricably linked. I am starting from first principles here, so those modellers who already have some experience may prefer to pass on to the next section.

The young modeller, keen to get trains running, will assemble their railway on the floor. This is great fun but it does not make a good choice for a permanent home. It is better by far to set it all up on a baseboard. This demands a degree of planning, and I would recommend anyone who is serious about the hobby to reach for pencil and paper before they even set foot through the door of a model shop. But when faced with a blank sheet of paper, it is easy to stray from a realistic design. When designing a railway, it is natural to reach for help in the shape of a book of 'plans', and there are plenty to choose from, but the modeller should beware. In many cases the plans were drawn in a way that ignores prototype practice, and any attempt to create an authentic-looking model, let alone proper signalling, is doomed from the outset. It is far better to seek out plans of actual locations to copy.

So what do modellers need to know before working on their railway, and their signalling system? First, the type of layout needs to be determined, depending on space and operating requirements. Second, for a truly satisfying modelling experience I would place the layout firmly in a geographical location, whether a railway actually ran there or not, and a definite historical period.

Layout types

Before starting, it would be as well to examine your motives for making the model, which will take a lot of time and (it must be said) money to complete. Are you after a lot of trains, running fast on a main line? Or are you more interested in shunting goods wagons? This, and the size of room available for your model, will dictate the type of layout you build.

Except under unusual circumstances, a railway line runs from A to B. You may see the same train twice after a while, but it will almost invariably be running back to where it came from in the other direction. Thus the type of layout known as the 'end-to-end' usually best represents reality. This can have a station at both ends or, if space is at a premium, the classic 'terminus to storage yard' design can be adopted. The storage sidings are where movement of rolling stock by hand is tolerated, and is often called the 'fiddle yard' in modellers' slang. If a through station is to be modelled, then two storage yards at each end will be needed to accommodate the trains. Signalling design follows normal procedure on this type of layout. With clever planning, using a spiral, perhaps, or a figure-of-eight arrangement, quite a lot of running line can be incorporated. A development of this idea is the 'out-and-back' layout, where the train runs over a reversing loop and is stored for a time before returning. The 'dumb-bell' takes this further, with a

Signals in the landscape 3: Sometimes in the urban environment all that there is to make us aware of the presence of a railway is a bridge and a brief glimpse of some signals, so closely do the buildings cluster around it. This claustrophobic impression is given by a street at 'Clarendon', the 4mm-scale P4 layout of the Leamington & Warwick Model Railway Society, which is set in the Kensington area of London in 1908. Tony Wright, courtesy of British Railway Modelling

Below: *John Hobden's interpretation of one of the Melton West concrete home signals, installed at Banningham on his 7mm O-gauge Norfolk Joint Railway. He has rearranged the arms to suit the geography of the layout, the splitting Distants being for Banningham Junction beyond the station. Great Northern-type somersault signals are notoriously difficult to model.* John Hobden

reversing loop at each end. If the room available for the layout is large enough, designs like this can be quite extensive.

Nevertheless, many modellers opt for the continuous-run approach, which has existed from the earliest days of railway modelling. This is, of course, not at all realistic, unless you are modelling the London Underground Circle Line! However, I admit that there is something satisfying in having a train moving continuously, even if it is passing the same location time and time again. The continuous run is the usual starting point for the first-time or younger modeller, but it makes the job of signalling much more difficult, as the signals for one location merge into those of another, and block working becomes more or less redundant.

A compromise is to have a hidden section where storage sidings are situated. The layout is still a continuous run and can be operated as such if required, but can also be treated as an end-to-end layout, with sidings assigned to specific destinations, where trains can be held until needed again. Under these circumstances the storage yard operator or operators can act as the remote signalmen for each end of the modelled section, and block working can work effectively.

Above: *Signals in the landscape 4: In the low-lying area around Retford, this gantry of signals approaching the flat crossing makes a distinct vertical landmark. This monumental layout, set in the late 1950s and early '60s, is being constructed by Roy Jackson in 4mm-scale EM gauge.* Tony Wright, courtesy of British Railway Modelling

Location

There are usually three geographical choices at the design stage: reproduce an actual location, model a location where the railway of choice might have run, or invent one – the 'freelance' option.

Modelling an actual location has the advantage that the trackwork and signalling are already designed, and research using Ordnance Survey maps and photographs will determine where the signals were and what they looked like. Diligent searching may even (if you are very lucky) turn up an actual signalbox diagram. In that case, I hope this book may help in the understanding of the reasons behind the design. The problem here is usually one of space, finding the degree of 'compression' with which you are comfortable; this 'compression' factor is dealt with in Chapter 6.

The second option will probably involve a similar process, as a typical station or other location for the

chosen railway company could be copied or adapted, as I did for 'East Walsham',
my OO-gauge 4mm-scale exhibition layout at present under construction. Here,
any spatial considerations can be eased by the utilisation of a 'history' that
explains the small site. For example, the station might have once been a 'light
railway', which was subsequently brought up to main-line standards.

The third option, going 'freelance', is probably the most difficult, and yet
perversely is the most common route followed by beginners. Whereas they are
free to invent their own railway, the number of decisions to be made increases, and
the making of them becomes more difficult and possibly erroneous by not being
anchored in reality. This is not to say that the freelance option cannot be
successful; in fact, many classic layouts of the past have been freelance, for
example the 'West Midland' system of Edward Beal, or John Ahern's 'Madder
Valley'.

Historical background

The freelance option allows modellers to run any locomotives and trains they like,
without being tied to a particular time or region. Some freelance layouts are set in
the 'preservation era', so almost anything can be run without comment. Whether

Ever mindful of economy, the LMS has reused these rotating ground signals, mounting new enamelled plates to show a lower-quadrant aspect for 'Proceed'. The signals are motor-operated.
British Railways, Ian Allan Library

More equipment surviving from an earlier age. A Grimsby-bound DMU has just passed Roxton Sidings on the ex-GCR line from Doncaster in September 1979, signalled by one of the last remaining somersault signals then in main-line service. The signalbox itself dates from the days of the Manchester, Sheffield & Lincolnshire Railway, the name that the GCR carried before 1897 and its ambitious extension to London Marylebone. The signal itself, lever No 17 in the frame, was probably installed in the mid-1920s by the LNER, using the Melton Constable design of concrete post.
L. A. Nixon

that is or is not a flattering view of the state of some of our preserved lines, I am not so sure. However, I would recommend that the modeller has a definite place and time in mind for the model, even if it is today and the line that runs past the bottom of the garden, or when they were 10 years old, trainspotting on a station. Then there may be an interest in a particular railway company to consider. All these parameters guide the design process.

To help those unfamiliar with the long history of railway companies to decide on a timeframe, I will give a brief historical overview here. As a rough guide, you can divide the history of railways into about six eras: early pre-Grouping railways (1840-89), established pre-Grouping railways (1890-1922), Grouped railways (1923-47), British Railways steam (1948-68), British Rail modern image (1969-94), and privatisation (1995-present). The most popular eras for modellers who prefer to use proprietary 'ready-to-run' items are those after 1923. The earlier periods lack trade support, so are usually the province of modellers who build from kits or completely from 'scratch'. Speaking personally, I am interested in reproducing as exactly as I can the appearance and working of a rural station in North Norfolk before the First World War. This can make things difficult, so if the amount of time you can spend on your model is limited, the more recent historical periods are probably the ones to go for. More pragmatic modellers may well end up choosing the Great Western Railway as their prototype, as the overwhelming proportion of trade support (unfairly in my view) is geared to that one company.

The benchmark dates are the Railways Act 1889, the Grouping, and nationalisation. The 1889 Act forced all railways to use continuous brakes on passenger trains, and fully interlocked signalling, and ushered in the recognisably 'modern' era of the railway. The Grouping of 1 January 1923 refers to the amalgamation of the dozens of private railway companies into four major grouped railway companies, as shown on the accompanying map. I have outlined the main constituents here because the signalling equipment and signalboxes of the earlier companies persisted throughout the Grouping period. In turn, the nationalised railway retained much of the identity of the four Grouped railways and their constituents due to the creation of similar Regions within it. In the following list, the brackets contain the commonly used abbreviations of the company names, and the numbers where they are annotated numerically on the map (see page 13).

The London Midland & Scottish Railway (LMS) consisted of the Midland Railway (MR), London & North Western Railway (LNWR), Lancashire & Yorkshire Railway (L&Y), North Staffordshire Railway (NSR), Furness Railway (FR), Caledonian Railway (CR), Glasgow & South Western Railway (G&SW), Highland Railway (HR), Maryport & Carlisle Railway (M&CR), Stratford-upon-Avon & Midland Junction Railway (SMJ), North London Railway (NLR, 26) and Wirral Railway (WR).

The Great Western Railway consisted of the pre-Grouping Great Western Railway (GWR), Barry Railway (Barry, 19), Cambrian Railways (Cambrian), Brecon & Merthyr Railway (B&M), Taff Vale Railway (TV, 18), Rhymney Railway (RR, 20), Neath & Brecon Railway (N&B), Rhondda & Swansea Bay Railway (R&SB, 16), Port Talbot Railway & Docks (PT, 17) and Midland & South Western Junction Railway (M&SWJ).

The London & North Eastern Railway (LNER) consisted of the North Eastern Railway (NER), Great Northern Railway (GNR), Great Eastern Railway (GER), Great Central Railway (GCR), Hull & Barnsley Railway

Below: Despite the date being 1985, the signals and signalbox at Northolt Junction are still resolutely Great Western. The signals are enamelled steel arms mounted on tubular steel posts, as latterly adopted by the GWR and British Railways (Western Region). Northolt Junction was where the Great Central Railway and the GWR parted company with a 'burrowing' junction at the end of the GW&GC Joint line from Ashendon Junction and Aylesbury.
W. A. Sharman

Above: The shape of things to come: A searchlight-type colour-light signal and junction indicator at the eastern end of Thorpe-le-Soken station during the electrification of the Colchester to Clacton and Walton-on-the-Naze lines in February 1959. The white diamond indicates that a track circuit is in operation.
Ian Allan Library

(H&B), North British Railway (NBR), Great North of Scotland Railway (GNoS), Colne Valley & Halstead Railway (CV) and Mid-Suffolk Light Railway (MSLR).

The Southern Railway (SR) consisted of the London & South Western Railway (LSWR), London Brighton & South Coast Railway (LBSCR), South Eastern Railway (SER) and the London, Chatham & Dover Railway (LC&D). The latter two had been managed as the South Eastern & Chatham Railway (SECR) since 1899. The Southern also incorporated the three railways on the Isle of Wight: the Isle of Wight (32), Isle of Wight Central (31), and Freshwater, Yarmouth & Newport (30).

The Metropolitan Railway (24) and the District Railway (25) remained independent until absorbed by London Transport in 1933.

Large jointly owned railways unaffected by the Grouping were the Cheshire Lines Committee (CLC – LMS & LNER Joint), the Midland & Great Northern Joint Railway (M&GN – LMS & LNER Joint), and the Somerset & Dorset Joint Railway (S&D – LMS & SR Joint). The M&GN was operated by the LNER from 1 October 1936.

After nationalisation on 1 January 1948, Regions of British Railways were formed. On the whole the new Regions inherited much the same areas as the former private Grouped companies, but there were adjustments, with some lines being passed to a Region different from the rest of their old group. This included the London, Tilbury & Southend Railway (LT&SR), which became part of BR's Eastern Region (ER) in 1949; the GCR, which became part of the London Midland Region (LMR) in 1957; and the S&D, which became part of the Western Region (WR) in 1958.

Regional branding was achieved by giving stations signage in steel enamelled in different colours, with corresponding colours on posters and other literature. The Eastern Region (dark blue) included the southern area of the former LNER (ex-GNR, GCR and GER lines) with the addition of the M&GN. The North Eastern Region (tangerine) was the north-eastern area of the LNER (ex-NER and H&B lines), and was absorbed into the Eastern Region in 1967. The Western Region (brown) inherited all the area of the former GWR. The Southern Region (green) included all the area of the former SR with the addition of the S&D. The London Midland Region (maroon) included most of the area of the former LMS, with the addition of the CLC. Finally, the new Scottish Region (light blue) absorbed lines from both the LMS and LNER Scottish areas (ex-CR, NBR, G&SW, GNoS and HR lines).

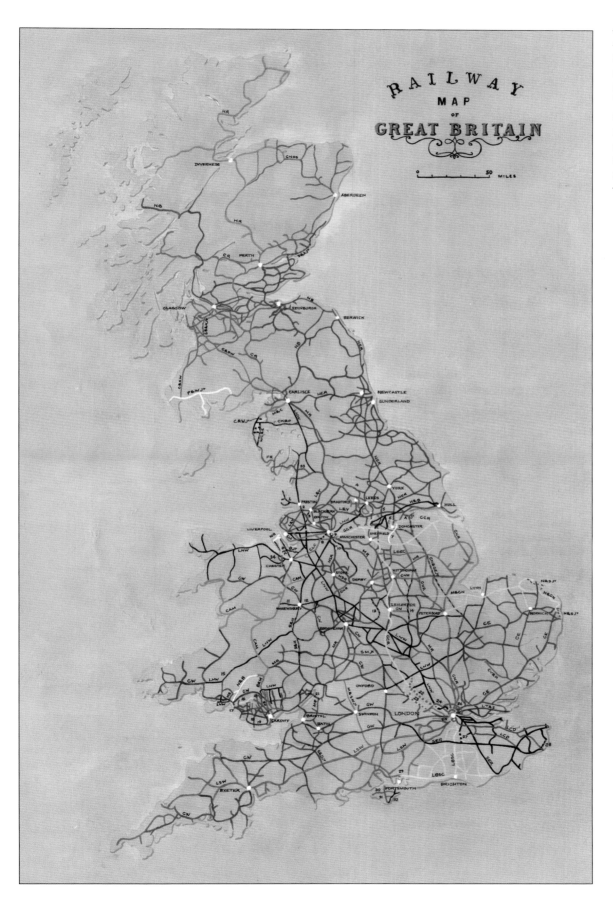

A map of the ownership of the railways of Great Britain before 1923. The companies are depicted by initials or numbers, with explanation and further annotations in the text. Author

Authentic planning

Having decided on your best options you can begin to draw your plan. Start from a general layout plan, then get into more detail. The length required to accommodate a set of points may be more than you think, so using squared graph paper is a good idea. Buy some points to work from, or consult manufacturers' catalogues for dimensions. The problems you encounter feed back into the overall design process. Once you feel you have evolved a good scheme, if possible draw it out at full size on a roll of paper (the back of an unwanted roll of wallpaper, for example), so that any final snags can be ironed out.

But if you are not directly copying from the prototype, what should you draw? Fortunately, there are a few rules of thumb that can be applied to any layout, whether it is a continuous run, an end-to-end, or a combination of both. The overriding consideration should be, I suppose, to keep it simple. Railways did not deliberately introduce complication in trackwork and its attendant signalling – it cost too much to install and maintain.

Although it may seem obvious, don't forget that British trains always run on the left-hand line of a double track, just as we drive on the left on British roads. There were a few locations with 'bi-directional' running, in other words two single lines side by side, such as can be seen today at Cromer.

Use as large a radius of curve as you possibly can. I try and have a minimum radius of 912mm (3 feet) on all my 4mm layouts. If you can't avoid sharp curves, put them where they can't be seen, and it may be better to gently curve your line or station than have an abrupt transfer from straight to curved track. Flexible track is obviously required for this, rather than preformed 'set-track'.

'Facing points' are to be avoided if at all possible. Unless a change of route was required, such as a junction, or a line diverging to another platform, connections between or onto double lines were required by the Board of Trade to be 'trailing'. On single-track lines, however, where trains run in both directions, facing points cannot be avoided. Facing points must always be provided with facing point locks, of which more later.

Outside 'station limits', any junctions traversed by passenger trains were required by the Board of Trade (later the Ministry of Transport) to be double line.

A plan of Cromer Beach station (M&GN), circa 1914, showing the signalbox (1), cattle pens (2), water tower and coaling stage (3), turntable (4), locomotive shed (5), goods shed (6), stables for collection and delivery of horses (7), goods office (8), goods reception road (9), headshunt (10), station building (11), facing points and facing point locks (12), trailing crossover for engine escape (13), Down Home signal (14), and Up Platform Starting signals (15). The Up Advanced Starting signal is off the diagram to the left, and there are a large number of directing Home signals on a pair of posts by the cemetery. Note other items such as gradient posts and mileposts.

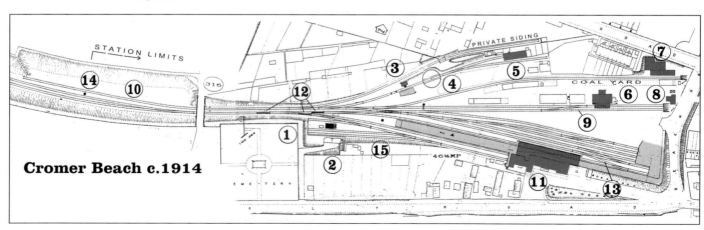

Cromer Beach c.1914

This applied even if the lines converging on the junction were single, resulting in just a few chains of double line to serve a double junction. This could be seen at Roughton Road Junction on the Norfolk & Suffolk Joint Railway (M&GN & GER Joint). This requirement was later rescinded. Junctions traversed only by goods trains could be single, such as Roade Junction on the SMJ.

Most small-to-medium-sized branch termini were adequately served by a single platform, with perhaps one or two bay platforms next to it. Multiple platforms were not needed, and actually made station operation more difficult. Where extra platforms were provided, they were usually only for occasional use, such as summer excursions.

At termini, or stations where services were timetabled to terminate, a crossover was almost always provided (trailing, of course) to allow the locomotive to escape and 'run round' its train, or make its way to the locomotive shed or servicing area. It was essential to release the engine as soon as possible for other duties. At larger termini, a pilot engine was sometimes used to drawn the empty carriages away to another platform or siding.

Where goods traffic was handled, it was often the case that a 'reception road' was provided, allowing a goods train to draw clear of the main line. At smaller stations this facility would be less likely, but invariably a line parallel to the main line and connected to the goods yard was provided, known variously as a 'headshunt' or 'shunting spur', allowing wagons to be shunted in the yard without interfering with the running of trains on the adjacent lines.

The accompanying drawing of Cromer Beach shows a typical small-to-medium-sized terminus, illustrating some of the rules noted above, and the facilities that the modeller could expect to be present at most periods of railway history.

Although Cromer has one, it is not strictly necessary to provide a goods shed. Many stations, particularly rural ones, did not have a shed, although there was invariably a small building that could be locked to store parcels and small consignments. This was usually referred to as a 'tariff shed', and was often sited on the platform rather than in the goods yard. This will help with the overall scene, as a goods yard should not look cramped, even if you only have a small space for it.

Finally, read avidly every book or magazine that might help you to depict your chosen period and location. Obtain Ordnance Survey maps, study photographs, join relevant societies, and search the Internet – it all helps.

The second signalbox at Cromer Beach, erected from concrete components in about 1920. For many years it was the only working ex-M&GN box, and since being taken out of use in 2000 has become a museum.
D. A. Digby

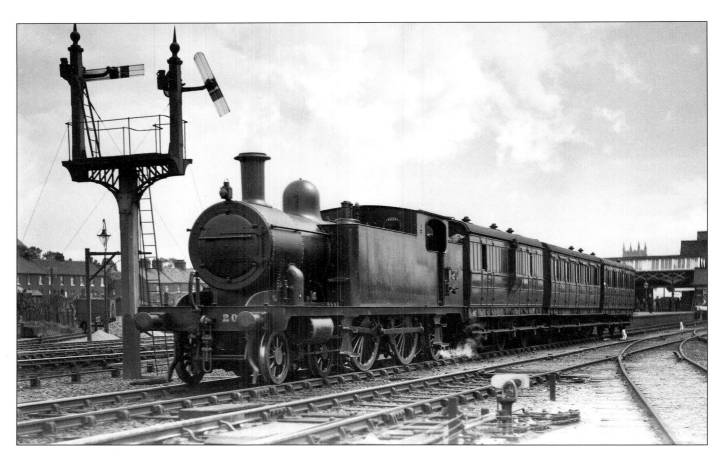

A classic view of an ordinary passenger train about to leave Cromer Beach circa 1932. The Starting signals have corrugated enamelled steel arms mounted on a traditional timber bracket post. The status of the train is given by the lampcode carried by the engine. The jaws of the tablet exchanger are folded out of use against the side of the engine. In the foreground are a number of signal wires and the chainwheels used to direct them, and an unusual somersault-type ground signal.
T. G. Hepburn

The engine escape crossover at Cromer Beach was operated by the small ground frame visible by the end brick pier of the trainshed. This was released from the signalbox. A hand point lever is in the foreground, beyond M&GN cattle wagon No 75. Note how the moving parts are boarded over. Locomotive & General Railway Photographs

CHAPTER

Basic principles

The prime object of signalling is to prevent collisions between trains by keeping them physically apart from one another. The simplest way of explaining this process is to compare railway signals to traffic lights, but whereas on the road a green light gives permission to proceed even if there are vehicles ahead, the railway green light or 'all right' indication is only given if the stretch of line ahead of it is known to be clear. Until recently this was achieved by dividing every line of railway into 'block sections', which were each controlled by a signalbox.

Protecting the block sections were the fixed signals. For the majority of railway history these signals have been semaphore arms. Originally, a semaphore signal was carried on a slotted post and could show three positions: horizontal for 'Stop', lowered at an angle for 'Proceed with caution', and out of sight in the slot in the post for 'All clear'. In addition, the section was considered clear unless a train was actually in it. After a terrible accident at Abbots Ripton on the Great Northern Railway in 1876, where the signal arms froze in the All clear position, these two previous conventions were superseded. First, railways adopted the familiar two-position standard for semaphore signals: horizontal or 'on' for Danger and lowered or 'off' for All clear. Second was the assumption of 'Line Blocked' as the normal state of affairs, with all signals at Danger.

'Stop' signals were positioned not only to give a driver an indication of when to stop but also where to stop, being placed to protect 'fouling points'. These fouling points could be the notional boundaries demanded by the block system, or more physical things like points or junctions, and were the places where vehicles could come into contact with one another. To give an indication of the state of the Stop signal ahead, a Distant signal was used, placed at a safe braking distance from the Stop signal. These were originally a variety of designs of rotating boards, but semaphores eventually replaced them. To distinguish it from a Stop signal, the Distant signal had a 'fishtail' or chevron cut into the end of its arm.

Lamps were supplied for night working, their colour being changed by the

The older way of signalling is illustrated by this circa 1881 view at Melton East Junction under construction, showing the signalbox and the Saxby & Farmer-type signals originally used by the M&GN's predecessor, the Eastern & Midlands Railway. The junction signals are mounted one above the other rather than side-by-side; the topmost arm will be for trains to Yarmouth and the lower one for trains to Norwich. Marriott Collection, courtesy of M&GN Circle

operation of the signal. For many years the lamps had been lower down the posts from the three-position arms, and Danger was shown by red, Caution by green, and Clear by the white light of the lamp itself. Lamps were originally fuelled by oil, but some were gas-lit, and later electricity was used. With the adoption of the conventional semaphore arms, a cast-iron spectacle plate was attached to the arm, carrying two coloured glasses. A white indication was still used on several railways for All Clear, although others began to use green. With a mixture of red, white and green, plus purple on some railways, the situation was dangerously confusing, and the Railway Clearing House (RCH) recommended the adoption of red and green only in 1893. As the light from lamps was yellowish, the glass colours supplied in spectacles were actually 'ruby' and 'cyan', which gave a bright red and a bluish green result respectively.

Originally, both Stop and Distant semaphore arms were painted bright red, with a white stripe or spot to aid contrast. The rear was painted white with a black stripe or spot. However, Distant signals became a real problem for the four railways created by the 1923 Grouping. The arms were fishtailed, it is true, but at night the red and green lights were the same as Stop signals. Some pre-Grouping railways, such as the London & South Western and the Great Eastern, had fitted Distants with Coligny-Welch lamps, which used mirrors to display a white chevron beside the spectacle lights at night. Experimental installations of three-position signals in 1914 and the first colour-light signals, all of which used a third yellow 'Caution' aspect, indicated the way forward, and from 1925 Distant signals were officially sanctioned (by the Ministry of Transport) to be painted yellow, with a black chevron on the arm and amber glass instead of ruby in the spectacle.

Another change after the Grouping was in the signals themselves. Until the mid-1920s most semaphores were lower-quadrant, pointing towards the ground when 'pulled off' to the Clear position. New semaphore signal installations would henceforth be upper-quadrant, pointing towards the sky when in the 'off' position. The Great Western Railway was the only railway not to adopt this policy, and later, when

it became British Railways (Western Region), the lower-quadrant remained the standard. The material of the arms also changed. Formerly, most railways used timber, but new arms were steel, stove-enamelled in the appropriate colour.

Colour-light signals started to make themselves apparent from 1920. The Southern and the London & North Eastern railways were in the forefront of this work, which made a significant alteration to the previous convention. By introducing a fourth 'double yellow' Caution aspect, a shortening of sections to give increased track occupancy was possible, taking advantage of the improvements in train braking since the 19th century. By the use of track circuits (see below), automatic working without intermediate signalboxes was possible, but the chief difference from earlier signalling was that these colour-lights showed green as the normal aspect. The signal just passed by a train showed red, and the three signals in rear of it displayed a single yellow, double yellow and green respectively. There were other designs, but by the mid-1930s the four-aspect system was seen as the future standard, except on the GWR, which contented itself with reproducing in lights the aspects formerly seen with semaphore installations.

Colour-light signals at first tended to occur on main lines, while on secondary routes the semaphore still reigned, although there could be isolated installations

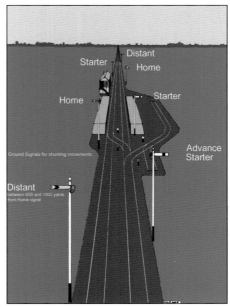

A snapshot of the usual amount of signalling that a modeller may need to provide. Taken at Reedham Junction in 2009, it shows the GER signalbox controlling BR (ER) upper-quadrant semaphores. In the distance is the Home signal, with the Starting signal in the foreground; there is also an Advanced Starter behind the photographer. The bracketed Starting signals in the other direction have the higher arm for Lowestoft, and the lower arm for the route to Yarmouth Vauxhall via Berney Arms. Author

A diagram showing the standard signals provided to work a station and the block sections on either side. The Advanced Starter is required to protect the next section from movements to and from connections in advance of the Starting signal, in this case the sidings. Author

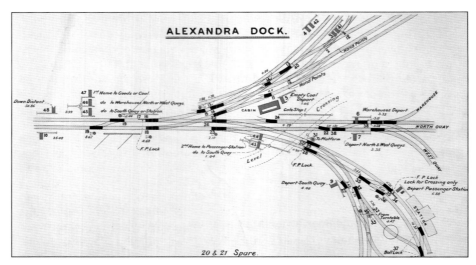

This beautiful work of art is the signalling diagram for Alexandra Dock signalbox, Hull & Barnsley Railway. It has many features that will be used or explained in the text. The black portions of the points show the way the switches lie when their levers are 'normal' in the frame.
Mick Nicholson

Ex-GER Distant signals near Wells-next-the-Sea, Norfolk, photographed in 1965, a year after the branch closed. The upper fixed Distant applied to the station itself, while the lower operated gate Distant applied to the level crossing over the main coast road. The post carries the remains of a McKenzie & Holland 'parachute'-type finial. A. A. Vickers

An evocative view of semaphore signals at night, showing the limited amount of light provided by the traditional spectacles of the ex-GNR somersault Humberstone Down Starting signal, on the outskirts of Leicester.
C. P. Walker

of colour-lights among the semaphores, often as Distant signals. Levers that controlled colour-light signals in otherwise conventional lever frames had their handles cut short.

Track circuits are a method of detecting the presence of a train by the shorting-out of an electrical circuit through its wheels. At places where a train is to be detected, the rails are made continuous for the required length by having bond wires fixed across the rail joints, which, until the advent of welded rails, were of fishplated and bolted in the usual way. At each end of the section, special insulating joints are made. Current from a battery is applied at one end of the track circuit and a relay at the other. When a train interrupts the current the relay opens, and thereby acts as a switch. This switch could either change an indicator in the signalbox, or change the aspect of a signal. Older rolling stock with wooden-centred Mansell wheels had to have bond wires fitted between the tyres and the axles to provide electrical continuity.

When track circuits were introduced in the early decades of the 20th century, they also allowed the relaxation of one of the most important rules, Rule 55. This stated that the fireman of any engine held at a Home signal must make his way to the signalbox and remind the signalman of his train's presence. Where a track circuit did this job by illuminating lights on the signalman's diagram, or by an indicator on the block shelf, a white diamond was fixed to the post of the signal concerned, showing the crew that Rule 55 did not apply, except if they had been detained for an unusually long time. Other methods designed to assist in following Rule 55 over the years were telephones, firemen's call plungers, treadles and electric depression bars.

Even though on some lines away from the trunk routes of the national railway system semaphore signalling still exists, colour-light signals have become the nationwide standard in recent years, and the remaining examples of semaphore signals are steadily being replaced. There will come a time very soon when traditional signals will be found only on the preserved lines or in museums.

The block section

The block section was the portion of line between the most advanced Starting signal of one signalbox and the outermost Home signal of the next, usually about 2 or 3 miles, but frequently more on minor routes, and on suburban lines often much less. The normal working was 'Absolute Block', with only one train allowed in the section at a time between two boxes.

It is important to remember that a signalbox, despite its geographical position, was not in the middle of its section. In fact, each signalbox guarded the entrance to the next section, which was nearby. Permission to enter the next section was obtained by means of 'block instruments' communicating electrically with the next signalbox, the one 'in advance'. Once permission had been given, the signalbox that had obtained that permission, the one 'in rear', lowered its Starting signal, allowing the train to proceed into the next section. Signalboxes were usually at stations or junctions, but where there would be too great a distance between block posts, resulting in reduced traffic capacity on the line, 'break section' boxes might

By contrast, the night-time view from the end of Platform 9 at Bristol Temple Meads is awash with light from the two-aspect colour-light signals. G. F. Heiron

The standard method of semaphore junction signalling at Gaer Junction, Newport, in 1959, with a Cardiff to Bristol Temple Meads DMU service passing through. Most of the signals have the later tubular posts and lower-quadrant enamelled arms, but the signal on the right is the earlier GWR type with wooden posts and arms. S. Rickard

The LNER signalling school at York in November 1930, showing an interesting mixture of semaphores and two- and three-aspect colour-lights, and a superb miniature 25-lever frame.
Ian Allan Library

be installed. Most of these became redundant with the advent of track circuiting, when automatic power-operated 'intermediate block' semaphore signals were installed instead, which were of course superseded by colour-light signals.

In theory, only one Stop signal was needed per section, but the practical requirements of railway operation demanded more protection for trains and more guidance for drivers. On approaching a signalbox, whether it was at a station or any other location, the first Stop signal the train encountered was the Home signal. This was placed in rear of the first fouling point. Where this was a direction signal for a facing point, the distance between the signal and the switch blades was usually a minimum of 60 feet, enough length to accommodate the facing point lock clearance bar (these terms will be covered in Chapter 4). The block section extended from the Starting signal of the box in rear to this signal.

At a distance of between 600 and 1,000 yards in rear of the Home signal, depending on the gradient, was the Distant signal. The interlocking of the levers in the box made it possible to pull off this signal only when all the Stop signals in advance of it were off.

A point 440 yards in advance of the Home signal was known as the clearing point, and a signalman was not allowed to accept a train unless his section was clear to his clearing point. Nor was he allowed to send the 'Train out of section' code to the signalbox in rear until a train had passed the clearing point intact, complete with its tail lamp. The Starting signal was often placed at the clearing point if there was sufficient length. At passing stations on single line, there was a slight modification of the principle, where a train could be accepted if the facing points were correctly set and the line was clear to the Starting signal, whether that was a quarter of a mile in advance of the Home signal or not. This had implications for the method of handling trains arriving simultaneously from both directions; in other words, to maintain the correct distance apart, one train would have to be held at the Home signal while the other was let into its platform, before being allowed in itself.

The portion of line controlled by the signalbox between the Home and Starting signals was known as 'station limits'. On highly occupied lines, the station limits

The platform starting signals at Norwich Thorpe in 1985, shortly before replacement by colour-light signals. The nearest ones are mounted on a standard BR (ER) steel post, but the furthest are on an older installation. Diamonds are fixed to the posts to show that track circuiting is in operation. The signals are accompanied by discs for shunt movements, and 'theatre'-type route indicators. Note the trap points and disc on the engine escape road. Author

could be extended by an extra Home signal provided 440 yards in rear of the Home, allowing another train to be admitted to the section while still preserving the clearing distance. The two signals were usually called Home and Outer Home. The station limits could also be extended by the use of Advanced Starting signals. These had to be used where there were additional connections from sidings or passing loops beyond the Starting signal, in order to protect the section ahead from accidental occupation resulting from a misunderstanding between signalman and engine crew.

Other signalling

Not all sites requiring signals were 'block posts', such as those within a section between other signalboxes. Some stations, particularly on single lines like the M&GN, consisted only of a single platform and a siding, and could not cross trains. In this case, only a small signalbox or cabin was supplied for the levers controlling any points and the signals protecting them, and sometimes they were in the open air. Repeaters of the bells, gongs, block instruments or tablet machines in the signalboxes at either end of the section showed when a train was in the section, and the porter-signalman (a recognised grade) would close and lock any level crossing gates and pull off the necessary signals. Some locations used an 'Annett's Key', which was literally a key in the lever frame, which when taken away to unlock the siding points locked all signals at Danger.

On main lines, level crossings were often provided with proper block signalboxes, but on secondary routes or lines where crossings were frequent and close together, this would have been impossible. The solution urged by the Board of Trade was to equip these crossings with Distant signals operated from a ground frame, but not all crossings were protected in this way, and many remained unsignalled. On the M&GN, crossings on curves or those difficult for drivers to see were equipped with Distant signals, but a high proportion (about 60%) remained without protection.

The gates themselves were considered as the 'Stop signals', and were provided with red boards of various designs. As long as the gates were set against road traffic the Distants were off, but to open the gates they had to be returned to Caution. It must be remembered that until the 1920s, with certain exceptions on very busy roads, it was normal for gates to be set against road traffic. Each gate was provided with a lamp with lenses at both the front and rear to warn road-users and trains alike. On the M&GN, gate lamps also had green sidelights, and drivers described journeys at night on certain sections of the line as being like 'an avenue of green lights'.

Level crossings normally had a gatehouse nearby, and it was often the case that a member of the permanent way staff occupied the gatehouse, and his wife was employed as the crossing-keeper. To make the staff aware of approaching trains, electrical repeaters showed the state of the instruments in the signalboxes on each side of the crossing, and bells or gongs also reproduced the communication between the signalmen (see Chapter 3).

Locations without signals

Many minor sidings on single lines were unlocked by using the single-line tablet or other token issued for the section, the ground frame being enclosed in a small cabin or even left in the open, no signals being required. Small ground frames were common at locations remote from the signalbox, but still within station limits. They might work the points at the entrance to some sidings, or more commonly, at terminal stations, to operate the engine escape points. Under these circumstances, the lever frame was locked by a bolt worked by a lever in the signalbox, or alternatively by an electric circuit. An indicator attached to the frame would read 'Locked' or 'Free' accordingly. Communication with the parent signalbox was usually by electric bell, using a code of rings.

An unmatched pair of level crossing gates at Thursford on the M&GN line near Melton Constable, showing what can happen after gates are damaged by a train or road vehicle. The Engineer's department used whatever material was to hand to make the repair. The further gate is the older, with the M&GN diamond warning target, but the nearer has the later LNER/BR round half-target. The lamp is an LNER type, painted red. The concrete gateposts are a Melton product, here painted white. Courtesy of M&GN Circle

The magnificent level crossing gates at Dogsthorpe near Peterborough. The unusual decision to use just one gate per side forced the manufacture of a very tall concrete gatepost. This is an original M&GN gate, with the hollow diamond warning board. The Home signal beyond the gate is an upper-quadrant arm fitted to a timber post that formerly carried a somersault signal. E. L. Back, courtesy of Michael Back

Identifying trains

As shown in the next chapter, signalmen communicated with each other electrically, and each train was described by its type – 'express passenger' or 'stopping goods', for example, to use the two extremes of train speed. It was important that all staff on the line were aware of the description of each train they saw. This was achieved by lamp codes. On the forward-facing part of the locomotive (smokebox when running normally, or rear of tender or bunker when running in reverse) a varying number of oil lamps were placed on brackets provided for the purpose. The number and position of these lamps conformed to a code describing the type of train approaching, which could be seen day or night. During the 19th century many railways had their own codes, and the M&GN conformed to the Midland Railway standard, using five lamp positions and two light colours, white and blue. However, from 1903 the Railway Clearing House issued a national standard of four lamp positions, which was adopted for most railways in white light only. This is a handy tool for dating photographs.

Not all companies followed this standard: the LSWR, LBSCR, SECR and Caledonian retained their elaborate codes. The LSWR used discs and diamonds in combinations of six possible positions; at night the discs were white lights and the

diamonds green. The LBSCR used two discs, one plain, the other featuring a cross, again replaced by white and green lights at night. The SECR adopted the old SER method of using discs and squares with various patterns to denote the route of the train, combined with lamps to describe the type of train itself. After the Grouping, the Southern Railway maintained this tradition of using discs. The Caledonian had probably the most elaborate scheme, involving green or white lamps and discs on each side of the locomotive cab, as well as on the front of the engine. In addition, a two-arm indicator, positioned rather like the hands on a clock, described the route the train was taking.

In 1918 the RCH lamp codes were altered so that only two lamps were used for any code, although there were still variations. During the 1920s and '30s the rise in centralised traffic control demanded a quick method of identifying certain passenger trains, and the use of 'reporting numbers' became common. These numbers were carried on brackets on the locomotives, and printed in the Working

Timetables or Special Notices so that signalmen could instantly identify them and telephone or telegraph their location to the Traffic Control Office. The reporting numbers were usually a combination of three letters and digits.

The RCH lamp codes were adopted by British Railways, but modified in 1950. Diesel locomotives carried them as discs during the day and lights (built into the body of the locomotive) at night. From 1961 the disc codes were replaced by a four-character code displayed in a box built onto the front of the locomotive, and the codes were modified again in 1962. This coding is still used, but after 1976 it was no longer displayed on the engines themselves.

At the rear of any train, an inverted triangle of red lights was required to show that it was complete. The triangle was made up of a pair of sidelights on the upper part of the rear vehicle – passenger or goods – with a lower single red light. The sidelights showed a white light facing forward so that the enginemen could see that the train was complete. When the train was turned into a loop or onto a slow line, the lamp nearest the main or fast line was changed to white facing the rear, indicating to approaching enginemen that the train was on an adjoining line. Sidelights on passenger trains generally fell out of use in the 1930s, although the LNER had abolished them in 1924. Goods trains continued to have sidelights, although the requirements for 'fully fitted' trains (those with a continuous automatic brake throughout the train) were reduced to one rear light from 1950.

There were additional lights on the rear of 'slip coaches' (vehicles detached from the rear of moving trains to serve a station where the main train did not stop), often set in red-painted boards. The rear of trains could also convey other messages. On the LBSCR a board lettered 'LV' (last vehicle) was used instead of a lamp during the day. At a time when popular trains had to be run in two or more portions, boards lettered 'TRAIN FOLLOWING' were a common sight, carried by the forward portion. All trains, be they humble diesel multiple-units (DMUs) or 'Eurostar', still carry red lights at the rear, and although the ubiquitous brake van is no longer used on goods trains, because all trains of wagons are now air-braked, all last vehicles carry a flashing red lamp.

The headcodes used over the E&M and M&GN, which from 1894 were based on the Midland Railway codes, and from 1903 were the standard Railway Clearing House codes. Author

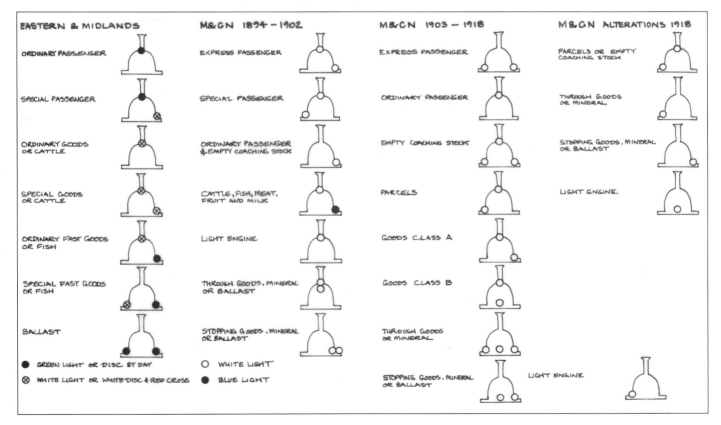

The Signalbox

A 7mm model of the original Cromer Yard Cabin built by the author for Lawrie Loveless. Author

Opposite bottom left: *The rear of Sleaford East ex-GNR box shows the reconstruction work that has taken place at two different times (the upper rear wall and under the windows), on both occasions with bricks slightly different from the original and each other. Author*

Opposite bottom right: *Working the levers at Ferryhill No 3 signalbox on the East Coast Main Line north of Stockton in June 1967. The world was listening to Sergeant Pepper but railway life carried on as it always had. This box was abolished in 1971. J. E. Hoggarth*

Components of the signalbox

The 'operating floor' of the traditional signalbox (where the lever frame was situated) was almost invariably elevated, usually one storey up, but sometimes more. This was to enable the signalman to get a clear view of the signals he operated, and the movement of trains. The operating floor was reached via a staircase, usually a wooden exterior one, but a few designs did have interior stairs. The room in the lower storey was the home of batteries for the block instruments, and was often the place where the signal fitters had access to the complicated interlocking mechanism of the lever frame. For this reason the room was usually called the 'locking room', even though some frames, such as those used by the Midland Railway, had the interlocking at floor level.

A typical design of mechanical box would have large windows at the front and sides of the operating floor to aid visibility, and the lever frame was usually at the front by these windows, although as time went on frames at the rear became

Right: *Cromer Yard Cabin circa 1900, its impressive height enabling the signalman, seen here holding a hand-exchange tablet pouch, to see over the adjacent bridge No.316. The bridge was demolished in 1920, and this timber box was replaced by a much lower one built of concrete.* Courtesy of M&GN Circle

Far right: *The cosy interior of Honing East M&GN signalbox as re-erected at Barton House, Wroxham. Note the shiny lino floor, the stove, and the lamp lighting the Train Register Book. The small window in the rear of the box allowed the signalman to see road traffic approaching his level crossing gates. Above it is hung the local gradient diagram.* Author

normal. Above the lever frame was the 'block shelf', on which the instruments were mounted. These included the block instruments themselves, bells, repeaters and the other paraphernalia of signal operation. On single lines the token instruments, such as tablet machines or train staff machines, would stand on the floor to one or both sides of the lever frame. If the box controlled a level crossing, very often a gatewheel would be squeezed in on the side next to the crossing so that the signalman could keep an eye on the road traffic while he closed the gates. Sometimes an existing signalbox was extended to accommodate new equipment, which could manifest itself as an extra, asymmetrical timber panel, or new brickwork. Modelling this kind of extension could add character and individuality to an otherwise mundane building, particularly if it is the kind of kit that many other people might have on their layouts.

To keep the signalman warm in winter, and to give him kettle-boiling facilities, a stove or fireplace was provided. Otherwise, the interior of a box could be rather spartan, unless the signalman himself brought things in to improve his comfort. In earlier times the floor might have been just bare boards, but in the 20th century linoleum became common. This was kept highly polished, as was everything else in the box, and woe betide an engineman or platelayer who entered with dirty boots! Hanging by the door in winter would be several heavy greatcoats for the use of the fogmen (see Chapter 4). Also by the door were coloured flags, ready to be grabbed quickly if needed.

Along one wall, usually the rear, were lockers for storage, but most important was the little desk, lit by its own lamp, on which the Train Register was kept. Every bell code and other incident during the day was recorded in case of accident or dispute. At very busy boxes, a lad was employed solely to fill in the register. At the beginning and end of each turn of duty the signalman was required to sign the book. For more serious occurrences, the details were written separately in an Incident Book.

Overlooking all this was the all-important clock. It was vital that the time should be known accurately in order to work the railway efficiently. A daily time signal was therefore sent down the telegraph or block bells (usually at 10.00am) and clocks had to be adjusted accordingly.

Signalbox design

The first structures that we would recognise as signalboxes began to appear in the 1860s, built by signal manufacturers such as Stevens, Saxby & Farmer and McKenzie & Holland, and later the Railway Signal Company. As the Board of Trade requirements for signalling increased in the 1860s and '70s, many railway

Top left: *Four Cross Roads signalbox was opened in 1891 as part of the interlocking of the line from Bourne to Spalding. The design has been dubbed by Michael Vanns the GNR Type 1b/Gainsborough (revival). The contract was let to the Railway Signal Company, and it is that company's design of bargeboard that adorns the gables.* P. H. Wells

Top right: *Yarmouth Yard signalbox was the largest on the M&GN, with 86 levers, and was opened in 1903. The M&GN Type 1a design was evolved in the Melton Constable drawing office, and has features common to both GNR and E&M practice. Three years later the vertical boarding was superseded by horizontal lapped boarding, introducing the M&GN Type 1b design.* Ian Allan Library

Above left: *The power box at Weaver Junction, north of Crewe, opened in March 1961 and incorporated a Westinghouse 'NX' panel. The cages around the colour-light signals were to protect staff from the overhead power cables, which have yet to be installed.* Ian Allan Library

Above right: *A new generation of signalman attends to the Cambridge station area of the GEC-General Signal 'NX' panel in this posed picture taken in the new Cambridge power box on 5 October 1982, two weeks before the panel was brought into operation.* Ian Allan Library

Above: *The new Derby power box is seen in June 1969, shortly before it was brought into operation. There is still a vestigial remnant of the traditional signalbox in the provision of some windows overlooking the railway; later designs dispensed with even those.*
Ian Allan Library

companies used these contractors to build their signalboxes, but they soon found it more economical to build them themselves. By 1880 most railway companies then in existence built their own boxes to more or less standardised designs. Some of the designs are shown in the photographs throughout this book, and Chapter 7 considers some of the available models.

From the 1890s there were improvements to the old mechanical lever frames by using 'powered' signal arms, allowing the levers in the signalbox to become merely switches, which could be miniaturised. However, the major development, in tandem with the adoption of colour-light signalling, was the use of electrical interlocking by relays instead of mechanical means. The way of the future was now 'route setting', in which the operation of one lever could automatically set up a complete route for a train, check for possible conflicts and 'prove' correct functioning all through the sequence. It was the LNER that revolutionised British signalling by opening the first route-setting 'panel' signalbox at Thirsk in 1933. Instead of the traditional bank of levers, all points and signals were controlled by switches on an illuminated panel. The final development was the 'entrance and exit', or 'NX', panel, where switches at the entrance and a push button at the end automatically set up the route.

Thirsk's elegant design, with a raised central control area seated on a larger lower storey containing the interlocking relays, was the first truly modern signalbox. Despite the new ability to replace several mechanical boxes by one new 'power' box, the Grouped companies persisted in maintaining traditional styling for their signalboxes. The Southern introduced its 'modern'-style box in 1935, but the GWR merely carried on using its former types, although the company did toy with flat roofs at some larger new power boxes, and the LMS mostly used a variation on the Midland Railway design with an LNWR-type gabled roof.

The Second World War forced all the 'Big Four' Grouped railways to adopt an uncompromisingly functional 'Air Raid Precaution'-style of signalbox, but ultimately the adoption of the panel freed signalboxes from their traditional appearance altogether and allowed the imposition of fashionable architectural styles on the buildings. This process, started at Thirsk, continues to the large 'Integrated Electronic Control Centres' of today, which do not resemble a signalbox in the slightest regard. The onward march of the IECC has meant that most of the thousands of traditional signalboxes, many of which were more than a century old, have been closed and demolished. The modern-image model railway need not have one at all, except perhaps as a derelict feature, or now in private ownership.

Signalbox communication

In order to find out if it was safe to send a train along the line into the next section, signalboxes needed to talk to one another. Before the days of the telephone, radio and electronics, signalboxes communicated by electro-mechanical means. The 'speaking telegraph' used a needle moving from side to side in a series of coded movements to convey messages letter by letter. Eventually, telephones were installed, but the single needle was still used until comparatively recent times.

The wires were taken along the lineside by the ubiquitous telegraph poles, which should not be forgotten. Note that the number of wires alongside many routes could be small, so the number of cross bars on commercially available telegraph poles may need to be reduced. Conversely, on main lines the amount of wires could be very large, requiring extra arms, and even sometimes duplicate poles. The poles were placed at 24 per mile, or roughly 70 yards apart.

It was realised in the 1850s that the single needle instrument could be adapted to show an indication of the state of the track in advance of the box, and several manufacturers brought out their own designs, the leading one being Tyer & Co. Other railways, such as the LNWR and GNR, had their own, and many GNR-type instruments were used on the M&GN. Although originally only two positions were shown, three positions – Line Blocked (the normal indication), Line Clear and Train On Line – became the rule after 1876. Many of these instruments used the same kind of handle as the speaking telegraph instrument, which had to be held over in its indication by a brass peg on a chain, hence the slang term 'pegger'; signalmen sometimes talked of 'pegging over' the indication. Other railways such as the Midland preferred a turning knob or rotary instrument, and some designs had a thumb catch. The repeater instrument, controlled from the box in advance, was often identical to the 'pegging' instrument, but without the handle, and was thus referred to as a 'non-pegger'. Some railways preferred to combine the two within the same wooden casing, and this did indeed become the general standard after Grouping. From the modeller's point of view, these combined instruments are most convenient. I will describe a simple way of reproducing the block instruments later.

As well as the needle showing the state of the track, signalmen had to alert each other to their needs in some way. To do this, single-stroke bells were used, activated by tappers or plungers in each signalbox. The M&GN arranged its instruments so that a signalman heard a bell from the box in the Up direction, and a gong from the box in the Down direction. Actually, the gong was a spiral of cast metal, which when struck by the beater produced a very pleasing 'dong', in contrast to the 'ding' of the bell. Where there were two or more block instruments from the same direction, the bells or gongs were tuned to different notes to aid identification. Some bells were exposed to view on the block shelf in the box, and highly polished; others were hidden in boxes or inside the block instruments themselves.

To ask permission for various trains or other requests, a code of bell rings was used. These were standardised by the Railway Clearing House in 1895, and subsequently revised in the 1930s and 1950s. I have given the most common pre-Grouping ones in a simplified form below, the numbers representing the beats on the bell, and the dash representing a pause between each group of rings:

Table 1: Code of Bell or Gong Signals (M&GN appendix 1913)

Call Attention		1 beat
Is Line Clear for...	Express Passenger Train	4
	Ordinary Passenger Train	3 - 1
	Parcels Train	5
	Express Goods Class A	3 - 2
	Express Goods Class B	1 - 4
	Through Goods	4 - 1
	Stopping Goods	3
	Light Engine or Engine and Brake	2 - 3
Train Entering Section		2
Train Out of Section		2 - 1
Cancelling Signal		3 - 5
Blocking Back		3 - 3
Section Clear, but Station or Junction Blocked		3 - 5 - 5

For the following brief description of the working of the traditional block system, we will assume that we have been allowed into a signalbox at an unnamed location, which we will consider Our Box. It is normal practice to refer to the signalbox from which a train is approaching as the box 'in rear', and the box to which we will send the train as the one 'in advance'.

a) Double line

The normal procedure for accepting and forwarding trains on a double line was relatively simple. The signalman at Our Box would hear the single beat of 'Call attention' from the box in rear, which he would repeat as acknowledgement (all

Diagrams of Indicators.

SEPARATE INSTRUMENTS FOR UP AND DOWN LINES.

FIGURE (i).

TRAIN ON LINE | LINE CLEAR

LINE BLOCKED

NORMAL POSITION.

Regulation 3 (a).

FIGURE (ii).

TRAIN ON LINE | LINE CLEAR

LINE BLOCKED

LINE CLEAR POSITION.

Regulation 3 (a).

FIGURE (iii).

TRAIN ON LINE | LINE CLEAR

LINE BLOCKED

TRAIN ON LINE POSITION.

Regulation 3 (c).

codes were acknowledged by repetition). Then he would hear another bell signal, asking permission for a train to enter his section, in the form of the appropriate bell code for the type of train being used. If the line was clear to the clearing point, our signalman could accept the train by repeating the bell code back, and would then 'peg over' his instrument to 'Line Clear'. The needle would point to the green portion of the dial, and a repeater in the box in rear would show the same. Once the train was on its way, the signal 'Train Entering Section' would be sent from the box in rear. After acknowledging that, our signalman would change his instrument to 'Train On Line' (which would also be repeated in the box in rear), and would set the appropriate points and 'pull off' the signals. On arrival of the train, and when he was satisfied that it had passed the clearing point complete, with rear lamp, our signalman would 'clear his frame' (replace the levers to their normal position), send the 'Train Out of Section' bell code to the box in rear, and return his instrument to 'Line Blocked', the normal position. This code would be repeated by the other signalman, and thus the line returned to its normal state, ready for another train. At each stage, an entry was made in the Train Register Book, so that there was a record in case of mishap.

Meanwhile, to send on the train our signalman would go through the same process outlined above to the box in advance. He would call attention, ask permission with the bell code and see the repeater in his box from the instrument in advance move to 'Line Clear'. The diagram shows this stage in the process. He would pull off the signals and allow the train to proceed, sending the 'Train Entering Section' code, and watching for the repeater to show 'Train On Line'. He would then clear the frame and wait for the 'Train Out of Section', watching for the repeater needle to drop to 'Line Blocked' before acknowledging it.

Of course, things did not always go to plan, and there were a variety of codes for mishaps, such as 'Obstruction Danger', 'Train Divided', 'Stop and Examine Train' and so on, but these would not normally come within the remit of a modeller. I have, however, included some more unusual but useful codes that need explanation. The 'Cancelling' signal was used when for some reason the train for which permission had been given or 'Train Entering Section' had been sent was no longer proceeding. The signal was acknowledged by the box in advance, and the block instrument returned to 'Line Blocked'. This is a very useful code

for the beginner! The 'Blocking Back' signal was used if a train or engine for some reason had to shunt outside the Home signal. Once it had been acknowledged by the box in rear, the signalman pegged the block instrument immediately to 'Train On Line'. When shunting was completed, the 'Train Out of Section' signal was sent and acknowledged as usual.

At a busy junction station or other location, the Traffic Manager of the line may authorise the 'Section Clear but Station or Junction Blocked' signal to be used when the line was clear up to the Home signal, but not beyond. This code was returned as answer to the request for permission bell code from the signalman in rear, before the block instrument was changed to 'Line Clear'. The signalman sending on the train would then know to caution the driver before he departed, so that he would approach the next box at a reduced speed. The rest of the sequence carried on as before. When the train reached the box in advance, the driver would find the Home signal against him until he had brought his train to a stand; then the Home (or a 'Calling-on' arm) would be pulled off, allowing him to proceed with caution.

A diagram showing typical double-line working in a signalbox. A train is in the section from Box A, and has been offered to and accepted by Box B.

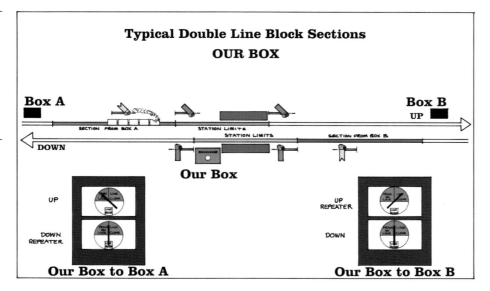

b) Single line

The working of single lines was the same in principle as for double line, but some kind of token such as a staff or tablet had to be provided to admit only one train onto the single line at one time. The two most common systems were Webb & Thomson's Electric Train Staff and Tyer's Electric Train Tablet.

Both worked in the same way, in that a single-line block section had one of these machines at each end of it, electrically linked so that the withdrawal of one of the metal tokens from one machine locked the other, thus preventing more than one train on the single line at a time. The train staff was a rod of metal marked with rings at one end arranged uniquely for each section, whereas a tablet was a metal disc provided with holes or slots for the same reason. For ease of handling, both sorts of token were generally placed by the signalman into a pouch with a large ring, allowing the engine fireman, when collecting the token for the stretch of line ahead, to put his forearm into it from a moving train.

On the M&GN, the Tyer's tablet system was used, the majority of the machines being Tyer's No 6, but also featuring some 'improved' No 1 types, modified by the company's works at Melton Constable to allow replacement of the tablet if necessary, as shown in the illustration. The process was the same in principle as for double line, using the same codes, but there were some operational differences because of the form of the tablet apparatus. Tablet machines were encased in large wooden boxes. Instead of needles on small dials, the tablet instrument had a large green reading face with two small windows, one for Up trains, one for Down. When

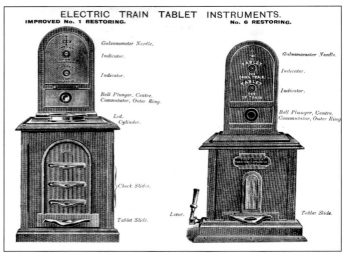

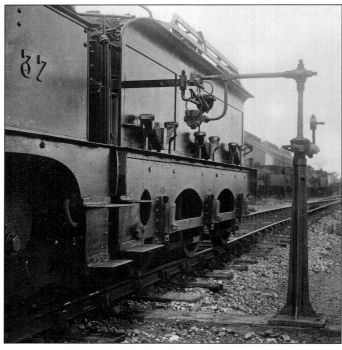

Top left: *The Tyer's Electric Train Staff machine in Pickburn signalbox, ex-Hull & Barnsley Railway, shortly before the closure of the branch in 1967.* Ron Prattley

Top right: *Engravings of the two different types of Tyer's Electric Train Tablet apparatus as used on the M&GN, taken from the M&GN Appendix to the Working Timetables No 3 of 1913.*

Above left: *The Whitaker automatic exchange apparatus being demonstrated at Highbridge Works on the Somerset & Dorset Joint Railway. The tablets are held in pouches with small hoops, which engage in the jaws of the exchangers. The S&D used push-out slides to mount the apparatus on their engines, but the M&GN preferred a folding approach.* Ian Allan Library

Above right: *Hand exchange of tablets taking place on the LMS. The pouches have much larger hoops to enable the arms of the signalman and engineman to pass through.* Ian Allan Library

Left: *A non-automatic tablet receiver at Roughton Road Junction in June 1961. The metal arm, wrapped in cord to slow down the hoop of the pouch, is tipped with a disc of white card for visibility, illuminated by a lamp at night. The wire cage prevents mishap. Beyond the receiver is a set of sprung catch points.* Ted Tuddenham, courtesy of M&GN Circle

not in use, both indicator windows showed 'IN' on a white ground. Beneath was a brass plunger surrounded by a commutator. At the top was a needle, which was deflected when the signalman at the other end of the section was pressing his plunger.

The first deviation from double-line practice was the lack of 'Call attention', made clear by the M&GN Appendices to the Working Timetable (WTT). However, by the British Railways period this signal was again being used. The signalman in Our Box would hear the bell or gong asking permission for a train to proceed into his section. He would repeat the signal using his plunger, on the last beat leaving the plunger pressed in for a short while. This was sufficient time for the other signalman to turn the commutator on his instrument anti-clockwise. This unlocked his tablet slide, and also made the appropriate indicator window in his instrument show 'OUT' on a red ground. He then withdrew his slide and took a tablet, giving a single beat with his plunger, causing the instrument in Our Box also to show a red 'OUT'. The tablet was then put into its pouch and passed to the driver to allow him to proceed.

If the timetable allowed it, our signalman could use the same process to extract a tablet for the next section in advance. The diagram shows this stage in the process, with the tablet for the next section waiting for exchange. Until 1907 an M&GN signalman would have placed the tablet in a pouch with a large ring for hand exchange, but after that date automatic exchangers were in use, and these pouches had special small rings to engage with the jaws of the apparatus on the ground or on the engine. If an engine not fitted with the apparatus, or one running tender-first, was to proceed through the section, an extra four beats were given after the 'Is Line Clear for...?' signal. This made the signalman aware of the need to use the hand-exchange pouch.

Once the train had been dispatched, the 'Train Entering Section' signal would be given and repeated just as for double line, but in tablet working no alteration of the machines was necessary. On arrival at Our Box, the tablet would be given up (either automatically or by hand) to the signalman, and the one for the next section exchanged where possible. Returning to the box, the signalman would lift the lever on the left of the tablet instrument to unlock his slide, then he would pull it out and place in it the tablet, face down, before pushing the slide back home. He would then give the 'Train Out of Section' signal, holding in the plunger on the last beat. This allowed the signalman in rear to turn his commutator clockwise, back to the normal position. He would then push his own slide home and repeat the 'Train Out of Section', giving an exaggerated last beat on his plunger. This would cause the indicator in Our Box to return to 'IN'. Our signalman would then send back one beat

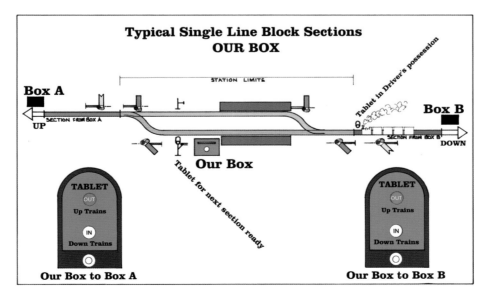

A diagram showing the working of a single line using tablets. A train is in the section from Box B. It has been offered to and accepted by Box A, enabling a tablet to be extracted and placed in the lineside apparatus ready for automatic exchange.

on his plunger, causing the indicator in the other box also to read 'IN'. The instrument was now ready for another train.

Just as for double line, things did not always go smoothly, and if the tablet had to be replaced without having been used, the signalman would put it in the slide face down, push the slide home, reverse the commutator and send the cancelling signal. Where a movement had to be undertaken beyond the Home signal (but inside an Advanced Starting signal), the blocking back code would be sent and acknowledged. This would be noted in the register, but no other action would be taken. When the line was again clear, the 'Train Out of Section' would be sent and acknowledged. Shunting beyond the Starting or Advanced Starting signals required two more bell and gong codes:

Release Tablet for Shunting	5 - 2
Shunting Completed, Tablet Replaced	2 - 5

The sequence of removing a tablet was just as before, and this locked up the machine at the far end of the section, preventing the approach of a train while shunting was taking place. Once shunting was complete the tablet was replaced as detailed above, with the appropriate code.

Other instruments

The block shelf wasn't only the preserve of block instruments and their bells – there were also repeaters and track circuit indicators. The signal repeaters were usually associated with Distant signals, which of course the signalman could not see. A switch on the signal itself made or broke an electrical circuit, the result of which was shown in the box, often as a miniature signal arm in a small circular glass-fronted case. Track circuit indicators were of a similar nature at first, where a needle, bar or semaphore moved to show that a train was on a particular section of track. Later, track circuits were often shown as lights on the signalling diagram over the levers.

Outside the box was a telegraph fault board, a shaped board usually painted white on one side and black on the other. This was a hangover from the days before telephone communication became normal. If there was a fault in the equipment, the signalman would hang the board with the black side showing, and hopefully a fitter would appear before long. Although superseded, these boards remained in use for many years. Various shapes were used: the M&GN used a diamond, the Midland an ellipse (painted blue) and the Great Northern a bell shape.

Modern single-line working

From the 1960s, moves were made to phase out the traditional single-line working using tablets and other tokens, and all of them involved the use of track circuits and treadles. Tokenless Block and No Signalman Key Token used relays to 'prove' that sections of line were clear before permission was given for a train to proceed. Further development came in the 1980s when Radio Electronic Token Block made use of computers and code numbers for each train to prove the section of line, with a token 'issued' electronically, and displayed in the driver's cab. Control Centres can now work large sections of single line in this way, removing the need for signalboxes at each crossing place. Where no colour-light signals are provided, fixed boards issue instructions to the driver.

Signal types

These very tall sky arms are at Dalston Junction, ex-North London Railway, photographed in 1937. The LNWR took over the day-to-day running of this line in 1909, and in keeping with this they are LNWR signal arms, probably on Stevens lattice iron posts. Co-acting arms are fitted lower down the posts.
Ian Allan Library

Signalling design

The organisation that forced development of signalling on the often reluctant railway companies was the Railway Inspectorate of the Board of Trade, later to become part of the Ministry of Transport. Some railways stuck to an absolute interpretation of the BoT/MoT Requirements for their signalling installations, while others were less dogmatic and relied more on hand and flag communication for shunting moves. The Great Western was well-known for the abundance and range of its signalling, with arms for just about every conceivable occasion, and the North Eastern was hardly less prolific. Railways such as the M&GN and the Midland were more sparing in their approach. Signalling alterations were undertaken from time to time, particularly in the Grouping and nationalisation eras, but it should be remembered that unless a situation demanded change, a signalling layout might survive for many years unaltered, with pre-Grouping equipment remaining in use. Modellers should therefore familiarise themselves with the practice of the particular company or BR Region in which they are interested. There are many books with photographs and other data regarding signalling, and of course there are the individual railway societies and the Signalling Record Society.

As we have seen, at the most basic level a Distant, Home and Starter signal in both directions was all that a signalbox needed in theory, but as well as telling the driver when and where to stop, a signal should also tell him where he is going. Thus it is very important for the enginemen to be able to see the signals, and in earlier times the sky was perceived as the best background for them, resulting in very tall posts, sometimes with co-acting arms or miniatures at eye level. As time went on shorter posts became more usual. To bring signals more into the eyeline of drivers where station canopies or other structures intruded, some companies, such as the Midland, were fond of providing 'underhung' arms, where the post was bracketed out and the arm was below the level of the bracket rather than above it. Where it was desirable to have the signal stand out in higher contrast to its surroundings, a white-painted sighting board might be mounted behind the arm, or a patch of brickwork behind the signal directly in the line of sight of a driver could be painted white.

The usual position for signal posts was to the left of the running line, but sometimes circumstances changed this. If a parallel headshunt or siding did not allow sufficient clearance, the signal post was placed to the left of this line instead. If a left-hand curve approaching the signal would prevent it from being seen sufficiently well, the post would be positioned on the right-hand side of the line. In locations where there were several parallel lines, the signals might be set above the line to which they applied by mounting them on a structure bridging the route, sometimes called a 'signal bridge', particularly if made of timber, but usually referred to as a 'signal gantry', and constructed of lattice ironwork.

Two arms for opposite directions of running on the same post was not an uncommon occurrence. These are two LNWR Stop arms mounted on the same post near Keswick on the Cockermouth, Keswick & Penrith Railway, photographed in 1965. R. L. Sewell

Distant signals

The semaphore Distant signal gave the first indication to the driver of the state of the road ahead. If the distant was 'off', then he knew that all the Stop signals ahead of him in the section were also 'off'. Where signalboxes were close together (three-quarters of a mile or less), the Distant arm for the box in advance was placed below the most advanced Stop arm of the box in rear in order to give the driver as early an indication as possible of any Stop signal ahead being set against him. Such Distant arms were slotted with the Stop arms above them; this slotting was usually an arrangement of three balance weights, which required both signalmen to pull the correct lever before the arm would fall. Two of the weights were each connected to one of the two signalboxes, and the third was the arm's balance weight; this was only free to move when both of the other weights had been moved. In this way, no driver would see a Distant arm 'off' below a Stop arm still 'on'. The Distant signals in rear of the 'splitting signals' at a junction originally also showed the same disposition of signal heights and arrangement as the Stop arms (see below) and were known as 'splitting Distants', although from the start of the 20th century this practice became less usual. Fixed, non-acting Distants were provided in some cases for the subsidiary routes, and from 1925 a single Distant arm sufficed.

Mechanical slotting on a post incorporating both a Stop and a Distant arm. Only by the lifting of both balance weights on the right by the reversing of two levers by two signalmen will the third weight, on the left, fall, operating the Distant arm.
Mick Nicholson

A slotted-post North Eastern Railway Distant signal, with the yellow arm and amber glass of the post-1925 railway.
John Hobden

Splitting signals

These were the multiple signals positioned at facing junctions to indicate the direction in which the points were set. Whether out on the line, or in the environs of a station, the same convention was adopted: what was considered the main route was usually given the highest arm, and the secondary routes had lower arms. These could be mounted on posts bracketed from the main one, or on posts next to it. The routes were displayed geographically, the disposition of the arms echoing the side of the main line from which the branches departed. In theory, if the two lines were of the same status, the arms might be at the same height, although in practice this happened only infrequently. The smaller posts carried on the brackets were called 'dolls'.

Junction signal arms were formerly stacked one on top of the other, a practice derived from the earliest days when signals were on posts over the roof of the

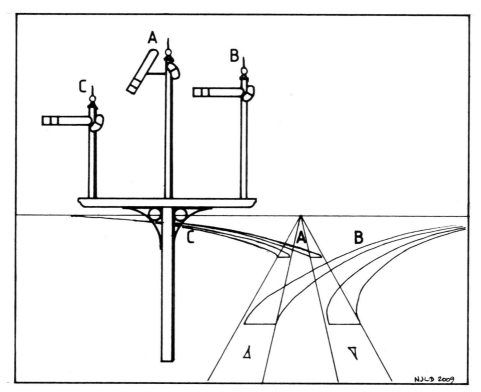

A diagram of the arrangement for splitting signals, showing the simple geographical correlation between the dolls and the branches to which they refer and the hierarchy of arm heights. The M&GN called these 'directing signals'. If the left-hand lower-status branch was for goods only, many railways would have fitted a ring to the arm.

signalbox. The convention was that the signals reading from top to bottom controlled the routes reading from left to right. The bracketed signal post largely superseded the stacking method in the 1870s, although it remained in use for miniature signals.

Subsidiary and miniature signals

Full-size signals were used for movements involving passenger trains, including junctions and lines into platforms. For goods trains and shunting movements, smaller signals were often used, usually with correspondingly smaller spectacles to distinguish the signal from a running signal at night. Many companies used semaphore arms, shorter in length than the main arms, for this purpose, and some made the distinction even more marked by fitting on the arms metal rings, painted white or black. The GER, GWR, LNWR and GCR were among those that employed rings on signals for goods lines. Neither of the parent companies of the M&GN followed this practice, so the Joint did not. The Midland had three sizes of arm, the main arm being 48 inches long (reduced from 60 inches circa 1900), a small one 30 inches long, and a miniature one 24 inches long from the spindle. The GNR was satisfied with two sizes, normal (60 by 10 inches) and miniature (30 by 6 ½ inches), and these were adopted on the formation of the M&GN in 1893. The former owning company, the Eastern & Midlands Railway, had used lower-quadrant arms in slotted posts derived from Saxby & Farmer practice. Some of these signals were

Right: The two lengths of arm used by the GNR and the M&GN – note that the pivot is in the upper half of the arm to encourage a fail-safe indication of Danger. These two timber arms were originally installed at Guestwick on the M&GN and are now preserved at Barton House, Wroxham. Author

Below right: A diagram of multiple miniature semaphore arms. The topmost arm refers to the leftmost route. Routes A, B and C are running lines controlled from the signalbox, even if they are only for goods traffic or shunting. Arm C gives permission to a driver to proceed onto the main line, as if it was a Starting signal.

Left: Stacked upper-quadrant miniature signals on 'Retford', the 4mm EM-gauge layout by Roy Jackson. Tony Wright, courtesy of British Railway Modelling

Below left: The same location as in the previous diagram, this time signalled purely as sidings. The ground signal gives permission to proceed on the main line only as far as the Advanced Starting signal, seen in the distance. Shunting takes place past the ground signal, which would once have been painted red, but after 1925 would have been a prime candidate for being painted yellow.

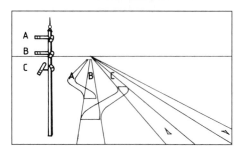

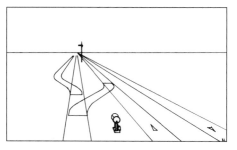

still in use ten years later, which illustrates the slow nature of change on the railways, and that one should not assume that obsolete equipment disappeared overnight.

Miniature signals were used on the whole for the exit from sidings onto a running line, or facing movements from a running line onto a siding. Once bracket signals became common, miniatures were the only types of signal that were still habitually stacked one above the other, the arms from top to bottom relating to the diverging rooms from left to right.

Ground signals

Ground signals are often overlooked, but were an essential part of signalling design. They controlled low-speed shunting movements and confirmed the correct setting of the required route. Most railways used a disc of some kind, but others had very small semaphores, while some had a Stevens pattern with a dropping flap. The M&GN used the GNR standard, which was a pair of discs with the lamp positioned between them, the whole rotating horizontally. In the pre-Grouping era the front face of a disc was red with a small red spectacle, the rear was white, and the rest of the signal was black. When rotated, the small white sidelight of the lamp was exposed. Ground signals had a variety of names, such as 'dummies' or 'dollies', but on the Joint line they were always referred to as 'Tommy Dods' or just 'dods'.

Two LNWR ground signals stacked one above the other, the uppermost one referring to the leftmost route as usual. Ian Allan Library

Top left: *A GNR-type ground signal at Eye Green, M&GN. The reading face is still painted red. The detector for the points is behind the signal.* E. L. Back, courtesy of Michael Back

Left: *An ex-Midland semaphore ground signal at Butterley, painted yellow and with amber spectacle glass. The 'printer's fist' indicates the line to which the signal refers. This design of ground signal originated in about 1910 from the MR's Signal Superintendent, W. C. Acfield, originally without the upper part of the casting, added later for visibility.* John Hobden

Right: Two LNER revolving-disc ground signals arranged to be read one above the other at Gilberdyke Junction, circa 1985. The white diamond indicates to the driver that a track circuit is in operation. Mick Nicholson

Far right: A side view of the same two disc signals at Gilberdyke Junction, showing how one is in fact behind the other. Gilberdyke Junction is on the ex-NER line from Selby to Hull. Mick Nicholson

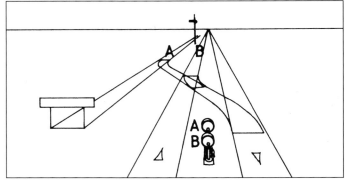

The exit signals at Old Oak Sidings, Willesden (LNWR), circa 1910. The lower arms on both posts are 'Shunt ahead' arms, fitted with a large metal S. Note how the shape of the S is painted on the rear of the arm. The signal lamps are gas-lit. In the background is Willesden Junction High Level station. This was part of the route of the North & South Junction Railway, linking the LNWR and the MR with the LSWR at Kew Bridge. There appear to be two LSWR engines in the yard. Ian Allan Library

Above: A diagram of ground signals sited one behind the other because of restricted space, but with the rear one having a taller spindle. The discs apply to wrong-road movements from the right-hand road only, and the usual rules of precedent apply. Disc A gives permission to proceed into the sidings, and disc B gives permission to proceed on the main line only as far as the Advanced Starting signal in the distance. Both discs would be painted red. If there were more room they would be arranged side by side.

Ground signals could be used in two ways. Primarily they were used for trailing connections where the shunt move was contrary to the normal running direction. A good example of this is a trailing crossover between two running lines; when an engine needed to pass from one road to the other, the driver looked to them for his permission. If more than one route was available, the discs might be placed side by side or one above the other.

Ground signals were also used for permission to exit a siding onto the main line if the points were in rear of a Starter or Advanced Starter. Normally, discs were regarded as Stop signals, but if that exit was a set of points from a headshunt, shunting might regularly be taking place past the ground signal when it was at Danger. This was officially tolerated until 1925, when the same MoT requirements that recommended the introduction of yellow Distants determined that discs in these circumstances should also be yellow. Adoption of this idea on anything but new work seems to have been slow, and even by 1933 the LNER (and by extension the M&GN) did not appear to be altering existing installations. The LMS was keener, issuing instructions in 1936.

Ground signals co-acting with a set of points or crossover were called point discs. They featured heavily on the E&M, and despite falling out of favour in the 1890s the M&GN did not replace them. Point discs did not give authority for the driver to move without confirmation from the signalman or shunter.

Not all railways were generous with their ground signals. The Midland provided ground signals for the exit of sidings onto the main line, as they were obliged to do, but frequently did not provide them for the reverse movement, which was cleared by flag from the signalbox. The Midland was a line that tried to keep its signalboxes small, by restricting the number of levers to the absolute minimum. This inspired the development of the combined economical facing point lock, and the provision of ground signals only where it was absolutely necessary.

Special signals

As well as the usual movements, there were special occasions that some companies thought deserved special signals. Prime among these was the 'Calling-on' signal, which allowed a driver to draw forward into a section already occupied by another train. This was called Permissive Block working (goods lines), or Permissive Platform working (passenger lines), where trains were able to share a long platform, as at Melton Constable. The Calling-on signal could simply be a miniature placed under the normal-sized Home arm, but many companies used distinguishing designs. The LNWR and the L&Y used a plain red short arm, and the GCR a very narrow arm with a white stripe. The LSWR and the Glasgow & South Western both used a diamond-shaped plate fixed on the small arm, but perhaps the most distinctive belonged to the GER and the Midland. The Great Eastern Calling-on arm was formed into an open diagonal cross, and the Midland arm was a 'T' shape, or 'hammerhead'. This arm was used by the M&GN, but in 'somersault' form. Colloquially, this was apparently known as 'going in under the hammer'. The GER open-cross signal had a cross shape formed on the green spectacle glass to aid in distinguishing it at night.

The cross-shaped arm was also used by the Caledonian, the North British and the LSWR, but as a backing signal, probably most famously at Midford on the Somerset & Dorset line. The GWR backing signal was a small red arm pierced with two holes.

Akin to the Calling-on arm was the 'Shunt ahead' arm, although this was intended for low-speed goods shunting and light engine movements only. In many cases, a small arm was fitted with a large metal 'S'. When lowered, the driver could shunt past the signal to an agreed point shown by a 'Limit of Shunt' board. The M&GN did not use this method of working until the 1930s, when two LNER shunt arms were installed at Norwich City.

Where a signal might be obscured from the driver's sight by a bridge, or a station canopy or other obstruction, a 'banner repeater' was often used.

This consisted of a circular glass-fronted case in which an electrically controlled black arm was pivoted centrally in front of a white background. When the signal to which the repeater applied was 'off', the arm rotated to a 45° angle, resembling a lower-quadrant signal in the 'off' position. If a Distant signal was being repeated, the black arm had a fishtail. At night a lamp positioned behind the arm illuminated the background.

Mechanical route indicators fitted to BR (WR) signals at Worcester (Shrub Hill) in June 1984. The signal applies to two possible routes and is worked from two separate levers, but the single arm drops for both. Note that the bracket signals in the background have fixed Distants. J. Checkley

Route indicators

In order to simplify some of the complicated arrangements of signals at stations resulting from the use of all the arms mentioned above, 'route indicators' were introduced from the early years of the 20th century onwards for low-speed movements. These had an illuminated background, against which cut-out metal letters or painted screens were displayed when the appropriate lever was pulled. Only a single arm above would be pulled off, but the letters would indicate the route to a driver. This cut down on the number of arms used, for example at St Pancras, the Midland's London terminus, where a gantry of 42 arms on 21 dolls was reduced to 16 arms on eight dolls with eight route indicators.

Lamps

Although there were instances of gas lighting for signals at night, and in the early days special candles were the standard light source, the majority of lamps from the 1880s were fuelled by oil. This was often called 'petroleum' at the time, although the word is now applied to motor spirit. The lamps were in two parts: an outer case equipped with lenses to focus the light, and the interior lamp itself. Both were fitted with plates carrying their numbers and the name of the signalbox and signal to which they were allocated. The lamp case usually had a small rear lens; this was the 'backlight', which helped the signalman see the indication of a signal at night from the rear. Each signal arm had a 'backshade', which obscured the backlight when the signal was pulled off, or, if fitted with a coloured spectacle, could show by its colour when the signal was off. On the GN and the M&GN this backlight was purple, and white was the indication when the signal was at Danger. Lamps for use with certain types of ground signal or level crossing gates might have coloured side lenses.

By day, the lamp interiors were removed and kept in a lamp room, where they were filled and trimmed, and only lit and mounted on the signals from an hour before sunset until dawn, or in conditions of poor visibility, fog or falling snow. This laborious task was only alleviated in the first decade of the 20th century by the gradual adoption of the long-burning lamp, which remained lit for at least a week and therefore only needed to be removed from the signal on a weekly basis. The GNR was an early user from 1908, joined by the LNWR in 1912. By the Grouping, most signals had long-burning lamps.

Since the 1930s there has been increasing use of electric lamps for signal lighting, but many surviving semaphore signals in network use are still lit by oil.

Post-Grouping standards

Shortly after the Grouping, for new semaphore work all the old company variety was discarded, and a new standard range of signals was introduced, of upper-quadrant form except on the GWR. There were two sizes of Stop arm, normal and miniature, enamelled red with a white vertical stripe in the usual way, and a special miniature arm with a horizontal white stripe. This could be left plain or fitted with a C as a Calling-on arm, or fitted with an S for a Shunt ahead arm. Ground signals were a white disc with a red or yellow stripe, which revolved in the vertical plane to show an upper- or lower-quadrant aspect. The GWR, of course, used the lower quadrant, and, strangely, so did the LMS. Of course, much of the older equipment survived for several more decades of use.

Colour-light signals

Despite the acceptance after the Grouping that the colour-light signal was the future standard, signal engineers were undecided at first how to apply the new technology. As a result, several types of colour-light signal were developed. The two main rival systems were the multi-aspect signal, and the 'searchlight' signal.

The multi-aspect colour-light signal was the most obvious method of design, at first using a simple vertical three-aspect display of (from top to bottom) green (Proceed), yellow (Caution) and red (Stop). This was a direct adoption of the display given by the three-position upper-quadrant semaphore signal common in the USA and tried at various places in the United Kingdom between 1914 and 1920. The LNER installed three-aspect colour-light signals over the former GCR line from Marylebone station to the new loop line at Wembley for the Empire Exhibition of 1924. However, the Southern Railway, when planning the extension of its third-rail electric system, could see that line occupancy would be seriously compromised if it used three-aspect lights, as the distance between signals still had to be dictated by the trains with the worst braking. The new electric trains had better braking, so the SR introduced a fourth aspect, the double yellow, which effectively enabled the length between

These colour-light signals on the Metropolitan Railway at Wembley Park were photographed in September 1932. The three-aspect signals are arranged in a junction pair, just as if they had been semaphores. The signalbox behind is the Met Type 4 design with a Westinghouse power frame, opened in January 1932. Ian Allan Library

Distant and Home signals to be halved. The light sequence was now green (Proceed), double yellow (Caution), yellow (Prepare to stop) and red (Stop). Steam trains would start braking at the double yellow indication, but electric trains could ignore this indication, braking at the single yellow light. First installed by the SR in 1926, the four-aspect method was subsequently followed by the LNER and LMS.

Because colour light signals were now spaced more regularly along a route, another signal, or for that matter a signalbox, would not necessarily be at the signal's clearing point. Although the concept remained, the minimum distance of 440 yards in advance of a signal was now often referred to as the 'overlap'.

The standard design of colour-light signal was to stack the four lights vertically, at first in the order of (from top to bottom) green, yellow, red, yellow, but by the 1930s this became yellow, green, yellow, red, which was inherited by British Railways and is still in use today. However, the SR and LMS were worried about clear sighting by drivers of signals suspended above the track, so they at first used clusters in these situations, where the four lamps were arranged in a cross, the two yellows vertically and the red and green to either side. This method was rarely used after 1929.

In the 'searchlight' type of signal, coloured lenses were not used, and instead a spectacle housing the coloured glasses was moved as required between the clear lens and the bulb. Two lamps were positioned one above the other. When four-aspect working was required, the bottom lamp could show all three colours, but the top one was yellow only, illuminated when the double yellow aspect was needed. The GWR preferred to mimic exactly the working of semaphore signals, so its searchlight lamps were placed the same distance apart as semaphore spectacles would be, and showed only two aspects each: red or green for the top lamp, and yellow or green for the bottom.

In slow-speed situations, such as approaching or leaving a station, route indicators were used above the colour-light signals. These were of the 'theatre' type, where small white lights were mounted in a square frame, forming letters or numbers when lit.

Where junctions were signalled, two sets of lights were provided at first, just as two semaphores had been bracketed to show a geographical relationship of the junction to the driver. From 1933 the LNER experimented with junction indicators on one colour-light signal. At first fluorescent tubes were tried, but soon afterwards a row of five small white lights was adopted, which remains the national standard today. The lines of lights, often called 'feathers', were angled to show the disposition of the junction ahead, and were lit only when the diverging route was being signalled. The SR used a line of three lights.

Ground signals could also be lights, but, unlike the main signals, the usual red and green indications were not used. Instead the LNER adopted what has remained until recently the national standard, a 'positional' ground signal. Three small lights are used. When Stop is indicated, a red (or yellow) and a white light form a horizontal line, but when Proceed is shown, the red light is extinguished and another white light above forms a 45° angle, the equivalent of a small upper-quadrant arm being raised.

Light Emitting Diode or LED lamps capable of showing all three colours, a return to the 'searchlight' idea, are now superseding the old style of colour-light signal. Ground signals are also being changed to LEDs, showing two horizontal red lights for stop, some with two separate lenses for the white Proceed indication, making four lenses in all.

Fog signalling

The advent of colour-light signals saw the decline of this special branch of signalling, already alluded to in Chapter 3. Because semaphore signals and their small lamps relied on good visibility, their indications had to be boosted by some method in fog or falling snow. This was brought about by stationing men at the Distant signals, called up for duty if an agreed point from the signalbox could no longer be seen. These fogmen were usually permanent way men, who would take their posts far away by the Distant signals, fortified only with bread and cheese. They were issued with greatcoats, flags and detonators; the latter were small explosive percussion caps, held on the rail by metal straps. If the Distant signal was at Caution, the fogman would place two detonators on the rail, which would alert the driver by their explosions that the Distant was 'on' and that he would probably have to stop at the Home signal. If it would be difficult for the fogmen to identify precisely the signals they were guarding, for example if the signal posts were very tall, or if there were many arms, small repeaters were fixed at eye level on the post.

To provide a modicum of comfort for the fogman, locations where fog was a common occurrence were provided with fog huts. These were simple wooden structures rather like a small sentry box. When out of use they were tipped forward and laid almost horizontally on the ground.

At some locations a degree of automation was brought in, so that one fogman, using levers or handwheels, could place detonators from machines at more than one place. At some signalboxes this was taken a step further by having levers in the lever frame for the placement of detonators from detonator machines, removing the need for fogmen at all. Colour-light signals, with their strong beams of light, made this universal.

A fog signalman, possibly on the Cheshire Lines, operates the fogging machine that places a detonator on the rail. Ian Allan Library

This detonator machine was once operated from the signalbox, but is now disconnected. Mick Nicholson

CHAPTER **Points and interlocking**

The Saxby & Farmer frame and the Tyer's No 6 tablet machine may make observers think they are on the M&GN, but in fact this is Cavendish on the GER Stour Valley line from Colchester to Cambridge via Haverhill, photographed in February 1967, a month before it closed. Much of the railway network was operated from hundreds of modest boxes such as this. P. Hocquard

The lever frame

The purpose of the signalbox was to protect the electrical equipment and to provide a sturdy support for the lever frame. The latter was the collection of levers required to operate all the points, signals, gate locks, facing point locks and so on installed at the location. The levers were long steel forgings, of which only about a half was visible above floor level; they were pivoted at their lower ends with a crank to impart a pull to a wire or a pull and push to a rod. The levers were mounted at a variety of spacings according to company (4 inches for some, 5 or 6 inches for others) in cast-iron frame 'standards', with the top part curved to follow the travel of the lever and a flat foot below that was carried on load-bearing beams or walls.

There were usually 10 levers to each standard, and curved floor plates or quadrants formed the slots that guided the levers. Handles were polished, and there were catches in a number of styles to retain the lever in position until pulled or reversed. To maintain the polish, a signalman never handled his levers directly, but always used his duster. Levers could not, of course, be pulled at will – they were interlocked, which ensured that they could only be pulled 'off' in a certain order, or when certain conditions had been fulfilled.

Each lever was numbered from 1 at the left-hand end up to the total number in the frame. The use of each lever was determined by a logical method: signals applying to trains approaching from the left would be at the left-hand end (starting with the Distant), and signals for trains approaching from the right at the right-hand end (ending with the Distant). In between were the levers for the points and facing point locks, and levers for subsidiary signals. Gate levers were at the end of the frame nearest the gates they released. The levers were painted according to function: green (from 1925 yellow) for Distant signals, red for Stop signals and ground discs, black for points, blue for facing point locks, black and blue for combined points and facing point locks, white for spares and brown for gate locks. Where detonator machines were controlled from the frame, these levers were painted with black and white chevrons, pointing up for the Up lines and down for the Down lines. An explanation of the layout was given in the form of a signalling diagram, framed and hung above the block shelf. Each lever's number, its function, and the numbers of the levers required to be pulled first were painted or engraved on a plate, either attached to the lever or positioned behind it at the back of the frame.

Below: A typical hand lever for changing points not under the control of a signalbox, at Eye Green, M&GN. The lever casting is mounted on point timbers and the moving parts are boarded over. The weighted arm is painted white. E. L. Back, courtesy of Michael Back

Point operation

Points (or turnouts) are made up from several items. The outer rails are the 'stock rails'; the moveable rails that turn the rolling stock from one route to the other are the 'switch rails', or simply 'switches'; the 'vee' where one route crosses the other is called the 'crossing', and the rails laid between the switches and the crossing are the 'closure rails'. What concerns the signalman most are the switch rails, as it is these that are moved by the levers in the frame. The switches are planed to a very thin edge at their 'toe' so that the wheels running on them progress smoothly from the stock rail onto the switch. The switches are attached and kept together as one moveable unit by the 'stretcher bars', a minimum of two, about 3 feet apart.

Left: *The workings of a conventional lever frame exposed in this publicity photograph for the Westinghouse Brake & Saxby Signal Co Ltd, a firm created in 1920 that incorporated most of the 19th-century signalling companies. The Saxby name was dropped in 1935. This 20-lever frame has interlocking activated by the catch handles, the locking tray being at the bottom.* Ian Allan Library

There were a number of requirements for points that might affect your signalling design. First of all it was good practice that, when levers were in the 'normal' position in the frame, points should lie set for the main running lines, and all other points should, where possible, lie in such a way that a runaway vehicle would be directed away from the main running lines. A crossover (a connection between one running line and a parallel one) would do this automatically, and it became usual for the points of a crossover to be double-ended and thus operated by a single lever. Where a single point was used, for example as an exit from a goods yard, a 'trap point' was installed, usually worked from the same lever. It was also desirable that trailing points were the norm, but at junctions, bay platforms or passing loops this was of course impossible.

In these cases the Board of Trade required that all facing points on lines carrying passenger traffic to be provided with a 'facing point lock' (FPL). This mechanism, usually operated by its own lever in the frame, was simply a bolt or plunger that pierced the stretcher bar when the lever was reversed, and prevented the signalman from moving the facing point until the bolt was removed by returning the lock lever to normal in the frame. As a precaution, at the same time that the bolt was being moved, a locking bar on the inside of a rail nearby was raised. If rolling stock was standing on the point, the flanges of the wheels prevented the

The narrow toe of a switch rail and the slender section of the stretcher bar almost defy one to model them. This close-up view was taken on the complex dock railways of Birkenhead in 1981. Author

At Prospect Hill Junction, Whitby, in June 1957, behind the photographer is the coast line to Scarborough via Robin Hood's Bay, which continues through the bridge to Saltburn. The link line to Whitby descends on the left, the signalbox being just out of view. Of interest are the catch points, which are signalled with a miniature arm and provided with a facing point lock. Ian Allan Library

locking bar from moving, thus preventing the release of the lock and the movement of the switches under a train. The FPL lever would of course be interlocked so that it had to be reversed before any signals could be cleared. The FPL mechanism between the switch rails was, fortunately for modellers, usually covered. The Midland Railway evolved an economical facing point lock that removed the need for an extra lever in the frame by combining the action of the switches and the FPL in one lever. This method was also used widely on the M&GN. Economical FPL levers were painted half black and half blue. The facing points at each end of a passing loop on a single line were designed to lie normally for the appropriate platform road, and the permanent way was usually laid out so that trains pulling into the station had a straight run.

Akin to the locking bar used in the facing point lock was the 'clearance bar', sometimes called a 'fouling bar'. This was again a bar lying inside a running rail, which was raised by a lever in the box. If an engine or train was standing over the bar, the wheel flanges would not allow it to rise, preventing the lever from working and therefore preventing the release of any levers in the frame that might cause a conflicting movement. This was used where engines or trains were in the habit of standing at platforms or junctions.

A facing point lock plunger and stretcher bar at Gilberdyke Junction.
Mick Nicholson

This official photograph was taken in 1945 to show the new 110lb flat-bottom-rail facing turnout laid in at Brayton North Junction, LNER, but it shows several other interesting points, such as the facing point lock, and the two NER ground signals of McKenzie & Holland type on the left. Ian Allan Library

'Detectors' were a method of ensuring that points had gone fully over before the relevant signals could be cleared. This involved the extension of a stretcher bar to a mechanism in which the control wire of the relevant signal moved a slide, which the stretcher crossed at right-angles. If the notches in the bar and the slide matched up, the point was considered 'proved' and the signal could be safely pulled off.

Some consideration has to be given to positioning a signalbox relative to the points it has to control. The original limit imposed by the Board of Trade was 150 yards in each direction, so a great number of early stations had signalboxes on the platform, halfway between the furthest points. The distance was relaxed to 200 yards in 1900 and 350 yards in 1925. Many stations were improved with new boxes positioned asymmetrically, by level crossings, for example; until then a small gate cabin would have been used to unlock the gates. In the 1930s the use of point motors extended the distance even further, so that at stations like Honing or Norwich City on the M&GN, one signalbox could be abolished and its points operated by another more than a quarter of a mile away.

Point rodding and signal wires

Outside the signalbox, the movement of the levers was transferred to horizontal pulling or pushing by the signalbox 'lead offs'. These were the cranks fitted directly outside the box, where the rods and wires emerged from inside through an aperture in the wall. Signalboxes built on platforms would have a low arch formed in the platform edge for the rodding and wires to emerge. Rodding and wires were concentrated neatly and economically in a run alongside the permanent way, leaving the run at right-angles where required.

The point rods, of channel section in the later Grouping and BR period, but of round section in the earlier eras, were carried to their points, clearance bars and other items to be operated by means of rodding 'stools'. These were low cast-iron frames fitted with several small wheels over which each rod would roll; at first they were mounted on timber stands to keep them clear of the ballast, but later concrete bases were almost universal. The rodding stools were able to force the rods in curves to follow the permanent way, but right-angled corners were achieved by the use of cranks. The longer the run of rodding, the greater the friction and the more difficult it was for the lever to be pulled in the frame. There were also losses in the amount of movement. To make up for this, compensators were fitted in long rodding runs, using linked cranks to restore the full throw of the rodding. These could be mounted horizontally on timbers, or vertically, sunk in boxes in the ground.

The pull from the levers was carried to signals by wires running on small pulleys mounted originally on short timber stub posts, although these were later largely superseded by concrete ones. Just as the for the point rodding, signal wire runs followed the curves of the permanent way, and large horizontal pulleys were used to turn right-angled corners; to prevent wear, the wire was replaced by chain at these pulleys.

The LMS Type 11c box at Broom North, formerly Broom Junction, controlled the junction between the Evesham to Redditch line of the Midland, and the former Stratford-upon-Avon & Midland Junction Railway. The junction had already had two Midland boxes prior to this replacement being opened in 1934, with an LMS frame at the rear of the box. It was renamed in 1942 when a south-facing direct line was built, visible on an embankment across the meadow in the background. Notable are the neat runs of point rodding and wires, the facing point locks, and the 'scotch block' across one rail of the line curving towards the turntable (out of view on the right).
M. Mitchell

Below left: A bell crank being used to turn the movement of point rodding.
Mick Nicholson

Below right: Rodding compensators at Gilberdyke Junction.
Mick Nicholson

Interlocking

Interlocking is quite simple, at least in its most basic form. Of course, it is not necessary for interlocking to be done on a model, but it adds so much to the enjoyment of working the box that I believe it should be seriously considered. I cannot pretend to know all but the simplest aspects of the subject, so readers must bear in mind that this is only the briefest of summaries, sufficient for simple layouts.

The purpose of interlocking is to interconnect levers in such a way that the action of one lever affects the other levers in order to:

> prevent a signal being pulled off until the road is correctly set;
> prevent the road in advance and in rear of a signal being reset once that signal has been pulled;
> prevent a conflicting movement being signalled or a conflicting road being set; and
> prevent a Distant signal being pulled off until all Stop signals in advance have been pulled off.

The interlocking was achieved in the majority of cases by connecting each lever to a long flat bar called the 'tappet', which passed with the other parallel tappets through a locking tray. Crossing the tappets at right-angles were the smaller locking bars. These had steel shapes, the locks, attached to them, which engaged with notches or ports in the tappet bars. The locks and the ports had bevelled edges, so that the movement of a tappet bar by its lever forced the locking bar to move sideways and affect other tappets. When a lever was reversed and the locking bars in contact with it were moved, a lock further along the bar either filled a port in another lever, preventing it from being pulled ('locked'), or vacated a port, allowing that lever to be pulled ('released'). One of the benefits of this method was reciprocal locking; in other words, if it was arranged that lever 2 locked lever 9 when reversed, the same mechanism made sure that 9 locked 2 when it was reversed. Another benefit was that if a lever released other levers when pulled, by locking that lever and preventing it from being reversed, those other levers were also locked; this was called indirect locking.

Both-way locking often applied to points in rear of a Starting signal, where two approach routes were available, but once the signal was pulled off the points were locked in position, whichever way they were set. This applied, for example, at East Walsham, where the Up Advanced Starter would lock the Down main points and the goods yard points both ways, as trains had three alternative routes to leave the station. The design of the East Walsham signalling is explained in Chapter 6.

Tappet locking was not the only system, although it proved to be the longest-lived one, being able to cope with the ever-expanding number of levers required at more and more locations. Some companies such as the Midland used a 'tumbler' system, and early Saxby & Farmer frames used a rocking bar and 'gridiron', a slotted plate. The locking in these examples was activated by the catch handles on the lever, rather than the lever itself, as were several designs of tappet-locked lever frames.

The locking frame

At first it may seem that a separate locking bar and channel are needed for each lever, but this is not so. In full-size practice, small-section rods connect the locks so that one channel can accommodate more than one movement. Both sides of the tappets can also be used, and reciprocal locking eliminates many locking bars. The locks themselves have different shapes according to their function. The lock that resides in a port when the levers are normal has a bevel at its top edge facing the throw of the lever. This imparts the sideways movement and is called the 'driving lock'. The other locks on the same bar are also bevelled on their top edge, which ensures that once the locking lever is returned to normal, the lever to which they belong drives the locking bar back to its rest position when it is pulled. The ports are, of course, shaped to fit the locks exactly. The both-way locks have a bevel at the top and bottom and two ports per lock. This ensures that they are locked in both positions, and can drive the locking bar back again from either.

Releases work differently. The lock and port on the lever to be released are shaped as before, with a bevel against the throw of the tappet, but the bevel and port on the lever doing the releasing are shaped with the bevel on the opposite corner. This ensures that the releasing lever, when it is returned to normal, drives the release lock back to its rest position. The port of the releasing tappet is displaced by a distance equal to the length of the travel, so that it is brought beside the lock when the lever is reversed. Only then can the lever to be released move.

It is obviously in the interests of everyone to keep the interlocking as simple as possible by eliminating duplication, and relying on indirect locking. This can often be achieved by considering the interlocking of the points first, as it is the convention that the road is set up before the signals are pulled off. Probably the best way to describe the method is to follow my working for the interlocking of some typical locations, remembering that for my own purposes and for the purposes of this book I am quite content to keep things simple. In the accompanying diagrams, drive locks are 'D', ordinary locks are 'L', both-way locks are 'B' and releases are 'R'.

First example: a double-line station

The plan shows a simple double-line station that could be found anywhere in the country, and the signals are provided in accordance with the concepts outlined in Chapter 4. The Up Home protects the fouling point where the crossover between the two main lines is positioned, the Up Starter being placed at the clearing point 440 yards beyond the Home. The Down Starter protects the fouling points of the crossover and the siding turnouts, the Down Home being place 440 yards to the rear of the Starter. An Advanced Starter protects the next section from trains leaving the sidings, and is placed the maximum train length (or 'berth') ahead of the points. Disc signals give permission for slow-speed shunting movements.

The levers are numbered in a logical fashion from left to right across the front of the signalbox. Notice how the point levers are sandwiched between the disc levers, which was a common arrangement. No facing point locks or clearance bars are needed for this layout. In reality, a number of spare levers would also be provided.

By considering each movement that trains may carry out, and looking at each lever and its effect on other levers, one can build up a locking table (Table 2). This is used as the template for designing the locking itself. Once the whole system has been analysed, the results are listed in the table. For example:

Movement 1: Into and out of the Down sidings. Reverse (5), which locks (8), (11) and (12) and releases (4) and (6). Levers (13), (7) and (9) are locked indirectly. Entering, (4) locks (6) and (10). Leaving, (10) must lock (5) points both ways and (4). (6) locks (4). Signals on the Up line remain unaffected.

Movement 2: Across the main line, Up to Down. Reverse (8), locking (2), (5), (11) and (12) and releasing (7) and (9). Disc (9) locks (3) and (7). Lever (10) must lock (8) both ways and (7). Distants (1) and (13) and discs (4) and (6) are indirectly locked.

Movement 3: Across the main line, Down to Up. Reverse (8), locking (2), (5), (11) and 12 and releasing (7) and (9) as above. Disc (7) locks (9) and (10). Up Starter (3) locks points (8) both ways.

Movement 4: Up trains. Signals (2) and (3) are reversed, locking (8), indirectly locking (7) and (9) and releasing (1).

Movement 5: Down trains. Signals (10), (11) and (12) are reversed, locking (5) and (8), indirectly locking (4), (6), (7) and (9) and releasing (13).

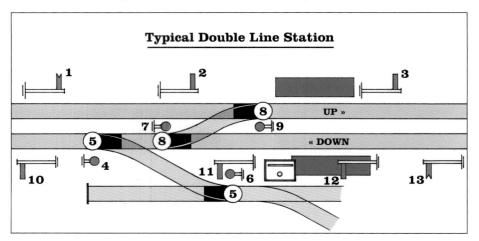

A diagram of a typical double-line station.

Walpole, a double-line station on the M&GN, is seen looking west towards Sutton Bridge in 1954. The Up Starter and the Down Home signals are apparent, the latter being a Midland arm on a concrete post. In the distance is a Distant for No 62 gates. Pamlin Prints, Author's collection

Table 2: Locking table, double-line station

Released by	Lever	Function	Locks
2, 3	1	Up Distant	
	2	Up Home	8
	3	Up Starter	8 both ways, 9
5	4	Disc Down Line to Down Sidings	6, 10
	5	Points Down Line to Down Sidings	8, 11, 12
5	6	Disc Down Sidings to Down Line	4
8	7	Disc Down Line to Up Line	9, 10
	8	Points Down Line to Up Line	2, 5, 11, 12
8	9	Disc Up Line to Down Line	3, 7
	10	Down Advanced Starter	4, 5 both ways, 7, 8 both ways
	11	Down Starter	5, 8
	12	Down Home	5, 8
10, 11, 12	13	Down Distant	

The locking chart, Table 3, shows the eight locking actions required for this lever frame, which can be accommodated in three channels, as in Table 4. The first channel could contain the functions of locking bars E, F, G and H, which don't overlap. Channel two could contain locking bars A and B, which travel in opposite directions and use each side of the tappets. Channel three could house locking bars C and D, which also travel in opposite directions.

Table 3: Locking chart, double-line station

Lever	1	2	3	4	5	6	7	8	9	10	11	12	13
Bar A					D			L			L	L	
Bar B		L						D			L	L	
Bar C				L	B		L	B		D			
Bar D			D					B	L				
Bar E							L	R	D				
Bar F				D	R	L							
Bar G	D	R	R										
Bar H										R	R	R	D

Table 4: Locking frame, double-line station

Channel	1	2	3	4	5	6	7	8	9	10	11	12	13
One	G	G	G	F	F	F	E	E	E	H	H	H	H
Two		B			A			A/B			A/B	A/B	
Three			D	C	C		C	D/C	D	C			

Second example: a single-line passing station

The second plan shows a typical passing station on a single-line railway, based on an M&GN station. The Down and Up Homes protect the facing points in either direction, being placed about 60 feet in rear of the switch rails to allow for the locking bars. The Starting signals are at the fouling points at each end of the passing loop. Advanced Starters have been provided for ease of shunting, so that a tablet need not be withdrawn, but these were by no means universal. Note that ground signals have been provided for the movements in and out of the siding, but other 'wrong road' movements used during shunting are signalled by flag only. The GWR and the NER would have used a great many more signals for this location. I have also used economical facing point locks for the sake of simplicity. A clearance bar is used at the fouling point of the Down facing points, because the signalman would not be able to see clearly if a Down train was fouling them for Up trains.

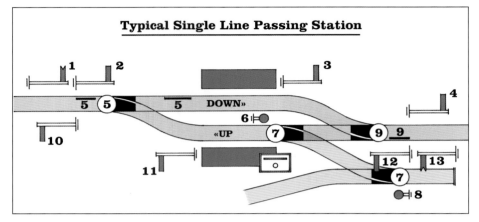

Movement 1: Arrival and departure of a Down train. Reverse (2), which locks (5) and (12). Levers (10), (11) and (13) are locked indirectly. If the train is departing, points (9) can be reversed, releasing (3) and (4). As lever (2) may have been returned to normal, (9) must also lock (12).

Movement 2: Arrival and departure of an Up train. Reverse (12), which locks (2), (7) and (9). Levers (1), (3), (4), (6) and (8) are locked indirectly. If the train is departing, points (5) can be reversed, as long as the clearance bar is unobstructed, which releases (10) and (11). As lever (12) may have been returned to normal, lever (5) must also lock (2). Levers (11) and (10) can now be reversed, locking (7) both ways, so that trains can leave from the siding as well as from the platform.

Movement 3: Shunting into the sidings. Reverse (7), which locks (12) and releases (6) and (8). These two discs mutually lock one another so that only one direction is signalled at any one time, and (6) must lock (11) for the same reason.

Table 5: Locking table, single-line station

Released by	Lever	Function	Locks
2, 3, 4	1	Down Distant	
	2	Down Home	5, 12
9	3	Down Starter	
9	4	Down Advanced Starter	
	5	Down facing points, FPL and clearance bar	2
7	6	Disc Up Line to Up Sidings	8, 11
	7	Points Up Line to Up Sidings	12
7	8	Disc Sidings to Up Line	6
	9	Up facing points and FPL	12
5	10	Up Advanced Starter	6, 7 both ways
5	11	Up Starter	6, 7 both ways
	12	Up Home	2, 7, 9
10, 11, 12	13	Up Distant	

The locking table (Table 5) can now be used to compile a locking chart (Table 6) of the individual actions required to interlock this lever frame. The design of the locking frame shows that only three channels are needed to accommodate the eight locking actions (Table 7).

Table 6: Locking chart, single-line station

Lever	1	2	3	4	5	6	7	8	9	10	11	12	13
Bar A		D			L							L	
Bar B							L		L			D	
Bar C						D	R	L					
Bar D							R	D					
Bar E					R	L	B			D	D		
Bar F			D	D					R				
Bar G	D	R	R	R									
Bar H										R	R	R	D

Table 7: Locking frame, single-line station

Channel	1	2	3	4	5	6	7	8	9	10	11	12	13
One		G	G	G		C	C	C		H	H	H	H
Two		A			A/E	E	E			E	E	A	
Three			F	F			D/B	D	F/B			B	

Third example: A double-line junction

Another typical railway feature was the double-line junction not associated with a station, shown in the third drawing. This example has the 'splitting Distants' associated with pre-1925 signalling, which mimic the 'splitting Home' signal protecting the facing points. The rest of the signalling is disposed as described in Chapter 4. In addition there are two clearance bars to ensure that an Up train has passed beyond the junction before the signalman can signal another along the diverging line. Once again I have used economical facing point locks for simplicity.

Movement 1: Up train on main line. Reversing clearance bar (7) releases (5) and (6). Reversing (6) must lock (9). Reversing (5) must lock (9) to prevent movement under train. Distant (4) is released. Levers 10 to 15 are unaffected.

Diagram of a typical double junction

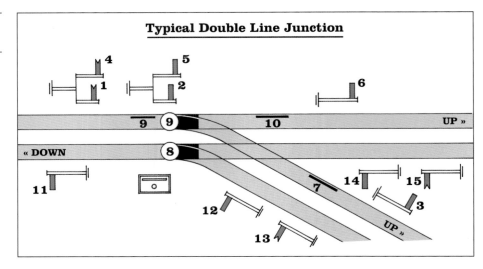

Typical Double Line Junction

At Runton West Junction on the M&GN in 1908, a GER train is coming off the Norfolk & Suffolk Joint line and receiving the tablet to proceed onto the single line, which continues to Sheringham behind the photographer. The signalbox is to the M&GN Type 1b design. Locomotive & General Railway Photographs, Author's collection

This complex of junctions is Benton Quarry Junction on the LNER East Coast Main Line near Newcastle, photographed looking north in 1946. Although many of the signal posts still carry McKenzie & Holland finials, all the semaphores are upper-quadrant. The immaculate lawn between the routes was later the site of the new Benton power box, opened in March 1964. Ian Allan Library

Movement 2: Down train on main line. Reversing (11) locks trailing points (8) both ways. Reversing (14) must lock (9), and (8) to prevent it being reversed under train. Distant (15) is released.

Movement 3: Up train entering branch. In order to reverse (9), (8) must be reversed, which avoids any possible collision by stock running away on Down line. Reversing (9) locks (5) and (6), and reversing (8) locks (14). Facing points (9) and clearance bar (10) release (2) and (3). Distant (1) is released by reversing (2) and (3). Levers 11 to 13 are free for Down branch train.

Movement 4: Down train leaving branch. Trailing points (8) are reversed, locking (14) and releasing (12). Starter (11) locks (8) both ways. Reversing (14) of course automatically backlocks (8), reversed to prevent movement under train. Distant (13) is released.

Table 8: Locking table, double-line junction

Released By	Lever	Locks	
2, 3	1	Up Branch Distant	
9, 10	2	Up Branch Directing Home	
9, 10	3	Up Branch Starter	
5, 6	4	Up Main Distant	
7	5	Up Main Directing Home	9
7	6	Up Main Starter	9
	7	Clearance bar	
	8	Points Down Branch to Down Main	14
8	9	Up facing points and FPL	5, 6, 14
	10	Clearance bar	
	11	Down Starter	8 both ways
8	12	Down Branch Home	
11, 12	13	Down Branch Distant	
	14	Down Main Home	8, 9
11, 14	15	Down Main Distant	

Although there are 10 locking actions on this frame (Table 8), they can still be accommodated on a locking frame of three channels by using both sides of the tappets and combining several locking bars in one channel (Tables 9 and 10).

Table 9: Locking chart, double-line junction

Lever	1	2	3	4	5	6	7	8	9	10	11	12	13	14	15
Bar A	D	R	R												
Bar B		D	D					R	R						
Bar C				D	R	R									
Bar D					D	D	R								
Bar E					L	L		R	D						
Bar F								L	L					D	
Bar G								B			D				
Bar H								R				D			
Bar J											R			R	D
Bar K											R	R	D		

Table 10: Locking frame, double-line junction

Channel	1	2	3	4	5	6	7	8	9	10	11	12	13	14	15
One		A	AB	AB	C	CD	CD	D		B	B	JK	K	K	J	J
Two						E	E		GE	E		G			
Three									HF	F			H		F

CHAPTER

6

Modelling the block system

This Midland Starting signal and MR Type 2b signalbox are at Butterley. The signal has the later cast-iron MR finial and applies to the route over the crossover to the parallel line, while the MR semaphore ground signal, painted somewhat anachronistically with a spot, applies to the straight-over route. The telegraph pole near the box was essential to take the wires needed for the block instruments; if the run of poles was on the other side of the line, a branch to the box was always provided.
John Hobden

The biggest obstacle to modelling an authentic signalling system is undoubtedly that of space. The average model railway is probably only 10 or 12 feet long at best. How then can the block system be incorporated when the minimum distance from a Home signal to a clearing point is 440 yards – 17 feet in 4mm scale, and 30 feet in 7mm scale? The answer is of course compression. It is a recognised procedure when building a layout to use shortening in a judicious and proportional way, in order to incorporate the features of a location economically. For example, the average length of a wayside station platform was 400 feet (5ft 3in in 4mm and 9 feet in 7mm), enough to accommodate an engine and six or seven bogie coaches, or 10 six-wheel carriages. If the maximum for the layout is set at four bogie vehicles and eight six-wheelers, then compression to three-quarter length can be achieved. With goods trains, further reduction may be

A drawing of the typical number of signals that you might need for your station, in this case a passing place on a single line. The Up Home signal in the foreground is situated to the left of the headshunt, there not being room for it between the lines.
Author

possible. The maximum length of goods trains on many lines like the M&GN was 60 wagons. Very few modellers can run these trains; the usual number of wagons is probably at most half that number. With this length now dictating the siding accommodation away from the platform area, further compression to about half the actual amount can be accommodated without spoiling that important ratio between train length and signal spacing.

A case in point is the plan of Cromer Beach, which is reproduced in Chapter 1. This is a popular plan to model, but the actual length of the station, from the foot of the embankment on Beach Road to the far end of the headshunt is 1,770 feet, or a whopping 23ft 3in (7,100mm) in 4mm scale. By shortening the platform and sidings, and increasing the curve of the approach, the plan could be accommodated in a room about 15 feet long, or, by using the diagonal, in a room a few feet shorter, but still retain the spirit of the original location.

Some modellers might wrestle with their consciences over even the slightest contraction and tightening of curves. Few

That rare beast on a model – a lone Distant signal – is seen here on the 2mm Finescale Chee Tor layout of the Manchester Model Railway Society, a representation of the Midland line through the Derbyshire Peaks in the early 1960s. Tony Wright, courtesy of British Railway Modelling

of us have the luxury of that choice, and I think, when weighing the pros and cons of compression, that we have to consider what the eye expects to see. By this I mean that more attention is naturally drawn to the immediate station area, and the more remote parts of sidings up to the buffer stops are not noticed so much by the observer and can be reduced accordingly. Nevertheless, whether one decides to reduce the length or not, the modelled signals are likely to be restricted to the Home and Starter in each direction. Distant signals are not usually required, unless they apply to a signalbox 'offstage', although this does not mean that an appropriate lever should be excluded from the modelled signalbox lever frame.

As well as being an essential component of the railway scene, the signals themselves can become part of the electrical operating system. The Reverend Peter Denny went so far as to tie in the signals and electrical supply so intimately that the locomotives on his renowned layout 'Buckingham' would not respond unless the right levers were pulled in the signalbox. On 'Dewsbury', the pioneering Scale Seven layout, the points and signals were locked both mechanically and electrically, nothing being allowed to move unless everything was correct. This does have its merits in that the operator is forced to use the signals rather than ignore them, but it would be difficult in situations where the movement was not a

Modern colour-light working on 'Runswick Leamside', the 4mm OO-gauge layout by Macclesfield Model Railway Group, set in 1989. Tony Wright, courtesy of British Railway Modelling

An evocative corner of 'Gresley Beat', the 4mm OO-gauge representation of the approaches to King's Cross station in the 1920s and '30s. The magnificent signals were built by Mick Nicholson, showing the standard method of erecting the signal on a baseplate.
Tony Wright, courtesy of British Railway Modelling

signalled one, being authorised by flag only. This circumstance happened more frequently than is thought by most modellers. On 'Heckmondwike', the first P4 layout, this problem was overcome by having a small light by the driving position, which the signalman illuminated to represent a hand signal.

The signal-electrical method would be ideal for the solo modeller, but it seems rather too rigid for my own taste. I think a driver should be able to pass signals at Danger just as in full-size practice, even if they do risk instant dismissal, or forfeit their cup of tea. Where I think that a certain amount of signal/electrical switching is appropriate is in the matter of driver change-over. One of the operating methods that I have adopted from Frank Roomes and his 'Lutton' layouts is the system whereby another driver (from the storage yard or next station) drives the train into your section, but you drive it out again. In this way an operator not only gets to watch a train moving on the layout and appreciate it just like any spectator, but also gets the pleasure of driving that train – the best of both worlds. This could be achieved by the lowering of a signal, which could be the Home or the Distant, the lever switching over electrical control of the section away from 'home' control to the remote or 'foreign' control. Another way would be to use the switching of the block instruments, as I have done at 'East Walsham'.

East Walsham station

Perhaps the most pressing task for many modellers is how to signal their stations. As we have seen in Chapter 5, an ordinary station on a double or single line is relatively straightforward, but there are usually additional facilities to complicate matters. So it was with East Walsham.

East Walsham, on the M&GN, is the working example I am using to describe the design of a signalling layout. This storage-yard-to-terminus layout is set in north Norfolk in 1906. The model has a full (if fictional) historical background and has been engineered in the style of the original contractor of the 1880s. My history has East Walsham, originally planned as a through station in 1880, in fact only opened as a terminus, the contractors Wilkinson & Jarvis turning their attention to another line. The terminus did eventually become a through station in 1907 in connection with the Norfolk & Suffolk Joint Railway extension from Mundesley through Happisburgh, and hosted trains from the Great Eastern Railway as well as the M&GN. I will model this phase of the railway's development at a later date.

The station of East Walsham as first opened in 1880 was quite conventional for the time. The signalbox, a small timber platform box used by the contractors at smaller locations, had a 14-lever frame from Saxby & Farmer, with three spares. Facing point locks had their own levers and the points to the sidings were only provided with point discs. The contractors saw this as quite sufficient, being concerned to keep levers to a minimum, as Saxby & Farmer calculated the price per lever. By the level crossing was a small cabin, which contained the levers that slotted the Down Distant and unlocked the gates, released from the signalbox.

The single platform was provided with a run-round loop, not signalled as a running line. The interlocking of the levers allowed the Home signal to be pulled off only if the points were lying normally, and the point discs at each end were co-acting. All signals were the lower-quadrant slotted-post S&F type as used on the Eastern & Midlands Railway. It is also worth mentioning that the permanent way was flat-bottom rail spiked directly to the sleepers and ballasted with sand and ash.

In my history of the line, the M&GN found it desirable in 1899 to resignal the station so that the loop line and the goods yard could act as reception roads,

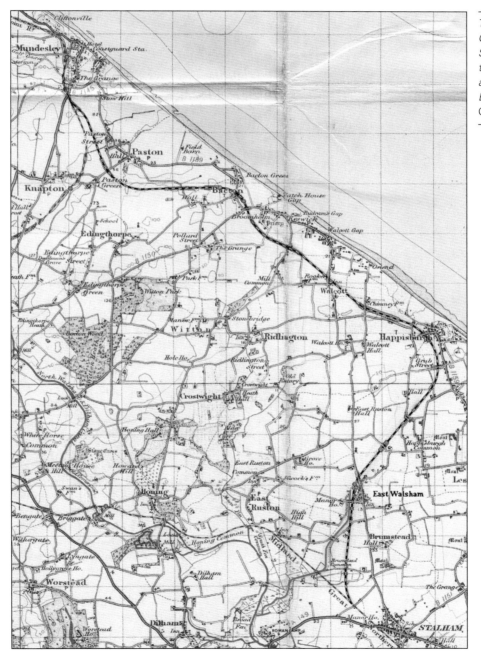

The 1945 edition of the One Inch Ordnance Survey map showing the Happisburgh line and the position of East Walsham. Crown Copyright Reserved

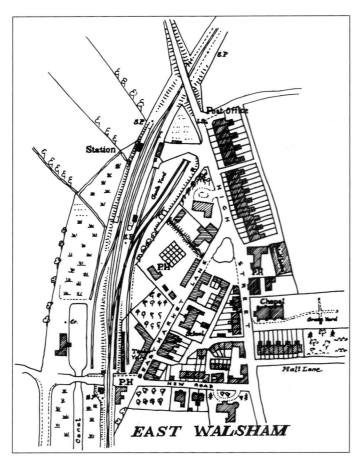

EAST WALSHAM

Very similar to the situation at East Walsham, here at Whitwell & Reepham (M&GN) we have the connection to the goods yard, the headshunt, the points where the passing loop becomes single line, and the Home and Starting signals, all in close proximity. The concrete posts have been painted white at one time with black bases, rather than left natural. Ian Allan Library

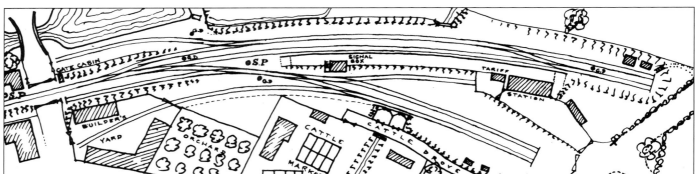

A drawing of the model of 'East Walsham', revealing the amount of contraction required to fit the plan onto the available baseboard. Author

allowing goods trains and passenger trains to cross. This actually happened at some M&GN single-platform stations, such as Guestwick. Another factor was preparing for the change to a passing station, the new line being authorised by Parliament. It was decided that the original signalbox was insufficient for the new work. A new signalbox to the M&GN Type 1a design was built further along the platform, equipped with a lever frame built by the M&GN from S&F parts and fitted with tappet locking. The old box was modified with a sliding door and used as a tariff shed. The opportunity was taken to replace the old E&M signals with new GNR-pattern 'somersault' ones, and GNR-pattern ground signals. Economical facing point locks were used throughout. At around the same time the main running lines were replaced by bullhead rail to the GNR pattern in 30-foot lengths, leaving only the sidings in the original flat-bottom rail. The only original E&M signal to remain was the point disc worked by lever No 7 on the canal siding. Note that Down on this part of the line was towards Mundesley and Cromer, opposite to the direction on the main line.

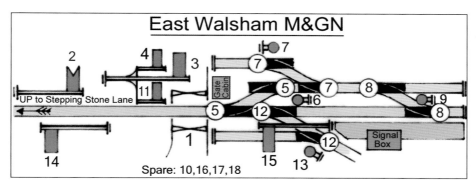

The signalling diagram of East Walsham, M&GN, 1899-1906.

Designing the track layout

East Walsham was to be a terminus, but I did not have the space to reproduce a Cromer Beach, or indeed a Yarmouth Beach. I needed something a lot simpler, with an explanation of why it was so simple, hence the potted history above. I wanted a station with the feel of Wilkinson & Jarvis's work of the late 1870s with the Great Yarmouth & Stalham Light Railway, so I decided that copying the layout actually used at Stalham would be a good start. I placed the location of East Walsham in a part of the parish of East Ruston on the Stalham to Bacton road, map reference TG365280. The contours of the land have been copied exactly and other factors have been added, such as the East Walsham branch of the North Walsham & Dilham Canal. The branch joined the main Stalham to North Walsham line of the M&GN at Stepping Stone Lane Junction.

A drawing of the fixed signals at East Walsham. Author

The maximum space I could allow myself for the layout was 12 feet (3,650mm) in length and up to 3 feet in width, although in the event I decided to keep the width to 2ft 3in (685mm) for access and portability. Using an Ordnance Survey map of the location, I planned out the whole alignment of the branch and the extension through Happisburgh to Mundesley. It became clear that the station would be on a curve, which was very convenient, as a gentle curve would utilise the available space efficiently, give an interesting line for the eye to follow, and leave space for the sidings behind the station. I then adapted the track plan of Stalham to fit the curve. From the 1/2500 plan, the modelled length of station was 1,600 feet, or 21 feet in 4mm scale. To fit the space, I had to reduce the whole station proportionally by about 50%, while retaining the overall appearance, which I think I have done successfully. The baseboards were divided into four 3-foot (912mm) sections, with 9 feet (2,740mm) modelled and the last board as the storage yard.

I arranged the geometry so that the line formed an arc between two tangents pointing towards the centre of the turntable-type storage yard to be installed at each end, allowing for future extension when I have more space. Of course, only one is required at present. The radius of the curve is approximately 14ft 6in (4,420mm), and most other curves are kept to a minimum of 3 feet.

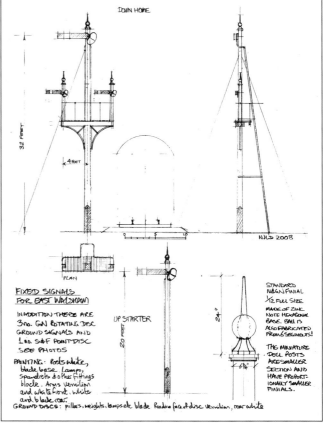

Designing the signalling

Before placing the signals I had to consider the future expansion of the station from single-platform terminus to double-platform passing place, so I had to design the full station first to get the right number of levers in the frame, even though some of them would be unused at first. This follows full-size practice, for example at Norwich City, where the contractor allowed several levers for the Norwich Central branch then before Parliament, but which was never built. I found that an 18-lever frame would be required for the through station, with as many levers as possible retaining their function before and after the alterations.

In the Down direction (towards East Walsham from Stalham), the first fouling point is the level crossing, followed closely by the Down facing points into the loop, with their locking bar. Naturally the Down Home signal is placed outside the level crossing gates. The Down Distant is 800 yards away towards Stepping Stone Lane, and as both it and the Stepping Stone Lane Distant would be near each other, I thought it likely that the M&GN would place both arms on one post, halfway between the two Home signals. The Down Distant signal is not on the scenic part of the layout, but its state will be shown to the storage yard operator.

In the Up direction, the first fouling point beyond the platform is the yard points. The Up Starter is therefore placed at the end of the platform to protect this. To protect the single line from the shunting that would have to take place, the Up Advanced Starter is placed a train length beyond the Down facing points. This means it is not actually on the scenic baseboard, but again, its state will be shown to the storage yard operator. However, I may fit a signal of under-scale size on the baseboard just in front of the backscene to give the impression of the Advance Starter being a long way off, as Frank Roomes did with one of his home signals at Lutton.

Now the main running signals were decided, I needed to look at subsidiary movements. The run-round loop was to be signalled as a running line for goods traffic, so a miniature semaphore had to be bracketed to the Down Home post to admit trains to it. In the reverse direction, a ground signal was placed at the fouling point of the trap points, controlling exit from the loop. The engine escape crossover was provided with a ground signal in the Up direction only, the reverse movement not being allowed, or indeed needed.

In order to signal the entrance to the goods yard, a second miniature was bracketed to the Down Home signal post, on the right-hand side. The opposite movement in the Up direction was controlled by another ground signal placed behind the fouling point of the switch rails of the yard crossover. As stated in Chapter 4, in this period of railway history all ground signals were painted red on their reading faces, whether trains ran past them or not – there would have been no yellow discs at East Walsham. Even when the line closed in 1953, I doubt that they would have been repainted or replaced by LNER types.

The placing of the signals was now complete. Assigning the levers to the signals and points was straightforward, starting from left to right with the Down signals and ending with the Up signals. The lever frame used from 1899 to 1906 had the functions as shown in the locking table (Table 11).

From 1907, when the station became a passing place, the only changes to the levers were: Down Starter (4), spare (6), Up facing points and FPL (8), Disc Up Main to Down Main (9), spare (10), Disc Up Main to Goods Yard (11), Up Home (16), and Up Distant (17). The miniature signal controlling facing movements into the goods yard was removed.

The level crossing gates are an important consideration, and must be interlocked with the signals. If the gates are open to road traffic, no signals can be reversed, and if a train has been signalled to arrive or depart, the gates cannot be opened. This is achieved by the Gate Release lever (1), which when normal locks the ground frame in the crossing cabin, and when reversed locks the signals in the station. On the model, this lever will be the actuating switch for the gate-opening mechanism.

Using the process outlined in Chapter 5, a locking table can now be drawn up (Table 11). The locking chart derived from this table (Table 12) shows that nine locking actions are needed for East Walsham, which can be accommodated in a locking frame using just four channels (Table 13). Looking ahead to the station in its later form, I discovered that the interlocking is actually much simpler, and could be easily accommodated in these four channels. The tappets and locks would have to be adjusted, but at least the locking tray itself would be large enough.

Table 11: East Walsham locking table

Released by	Lever	Function	Locks
	1	Gate Release	3, 5, 12, 14, 15
3	2	Down Distant	
	3	Down Home	1, 5, 8, 12, 14, 15
5	4	Miniature Main Line to Loop	6, 14
	5	Facing points Main Line to Loop and FPL	1, 3, 7, 12, 15
5	6	Disc Loop to Main	4
	7	Points and Disc to Canal Siding	5
	8	Points Platform Line to Loop	3, 15
8	9	Disc Platform Line to Loop	
12	10	Miniature Main Line to Up Sidings	13, 14
	11	Spare	
	12	Facing points Main Line to Up Sidings and FPL	1, 3, 5, 15
12	13	Disc Up Sidings to Main Line	10
	14	Up Advance Starter	1, 3, 4, 5 both ways, 10, 12 both ways
	15	Up Starter	1, 3, 5, 8, 12
	16	Spare	
	17	Spare	
	18	Spare	

Table 12: East Walsham locking chart

Lever	1	2	3	4	5	6	7	8	9	10	11	12	13	14	15
Bar A	D		L		L							L		L	L
Bar B			L		L			L				L			D
Bar C			D					L				L		L	L
Bar D								L				L			D
Bar E				L	B					L		B		D	
Bar F				D	R	L									
Bar G					R	D									
Bar H										D			R	L	
Bar J												R		D	

Table 13: East Walsham locking frame

Channel	1	2	3	4	5	6	7	8	9	10	11	12	13	14	15
One	A		A	F	F/A	F				H		H/A	H	A	A
Two			B		B			B/D				B/D			D/B
Three			C		G	G		C				C/J	J	C	C
Four				E	E			E				E		E	

Taking all these precautions ensures that East Walsham can function as a passing place, with two trains and their locomotives present in safety. This makes for more interesting working; although two passenger trains cannot cross, a passenger train can cross a goods train.

Stepping Stone Lane Junction

The branch leaves the Stalham to North Walsham section of the M&GN north of Stalham at Stepping Stone Lane Junction. As required for passenger traffic, the junction is 'double' – the single line doubles up before the second route leaves it. As the distance between Stalham and the junction is so small, 36 chains, or just less than half a mile, the line to the junction is double anyway, then becomes single beyond the junction on both main and branch lines. Just before the junction is level crossing No 32, which was given a gatehouse, although the junction signalbox was built only a year later (1881).

The diagram shows the track arrangement, the way the point switches lie when 'normal' to avoid route conflicts, and the facing point locks. It also shows the

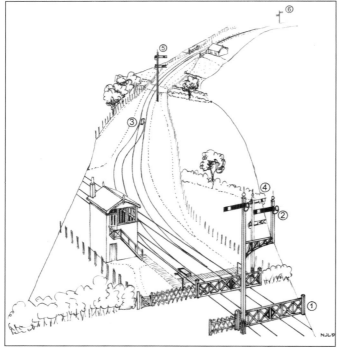

A drawing of the future modelled appearance of Stepping Stone Lane Junction. Author

typical signalling required to protect this junction. On the Stalham side of the crossing is the Up splitting signal, with the main-line arm higher than the branch. If the line between Stalham and the junction were single, the same Home signal would be positioned on the single line just before the facing points. The splitting Distants for this signal are on the Stalham Up Starter and Up Home, slotted with them, as the distance between the two Home signals is less than three-quarters of a mile. The diagram shows the conventional symbol for slotting, where a 'ghost' arm is drawn at 45 degrees to the Distant arm. As the points from double to single line are only a short distance beyond the Stepping Stone Lane junction points, there would be no point in placing any Up Starters there, so the splitting signals are the Starters as well as the Home, protecting the change to single line on main and branch.

In the Down direction (towards Stalham and Yarmouth Beach), the Down Homes guard both facing points and the Down Starter protects the entry to the Stalham section, just before the crossing gates. Below these arms are the Stalham Down Distants, slotted with the arms above. The junction Down Main Distant is 800 yards down the gradient towards

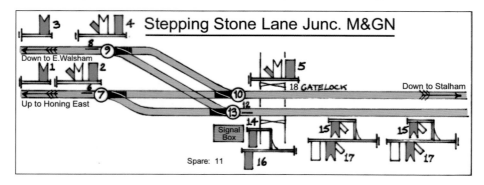

The signalling diagram of Stepping Stone Lane Junction.

crossing No 31, and the branch Distant a similar distance towards East Walsham. This junction is typical of hundreds all over the country, and could be reproduced for any layout, with suitable adjustments regarding the Distant signals.

The lever numbers are arranged in a typical order across the front of the signalbox, starting with the Down signals (Up from the branch) on the left of the frame, and ending with the Up signals on the right. As no shunting movements would be required, or engines standing waiting, I do not think that clearance bars would be used in the layout. The Gate Release lever would have unlocked the level crossing gates, locking the signals at Danger and allowing the signalman to use the gatewheel to open the gates to road traffic.

The levers are: Branch Up Distant (1), Branch Up Home (2), Down Main Distant (3), Down Main Home (4), Down Starter (5), Branch Up facing points and economical FPL (6), Down Main facing points and economical FPL (7), junction trailing points (8), junction facing points and economical FPL (9), Up Main splitting signal (10), Up Main splitting Distant (11), Up splitting signal to Branch (12), Up splitting Distant to Branch (13), and Gate Release (14). In reality, level crossings such as this often had wicket gates at one side for pedestrians, and these were usually also released and locked by a lever each.

Adapting the lever frame

If I ever expand the layout of East Walsham to Stepping Stone Lane Junction, the main-line part of it would be a dummy and only the branch would be functional. This illustrates one difficulty of modelling signalling – the position of your lever frame and the number of signals you need may be different from the prototype. Distant signals are often redundant on a model, as are facing point locks. Other levers such as detonator placers, clearance bars and, indeed, spares may also be omitted.

The main changes for the modelled version of Stepping Stone Lane Junction are that the operator will be on the opposite side from the signalbox and therefore the levers will have to be renumbered, and that all but one facing point and one Distant are not needed, a total saving of eight levers. The model lever frame could be numbered as shown in the illustration:

Stepping Stone Lane Junction
1 Gate Release
2 Up splitting signal to Branch
3 Branch Up facing points
4 Down Main Starter
5 Branch Up Home
6 Branch Up Distant

The gate lever would be a switch used to activate the gate mechanism.

A beautiful example of a double-line junction on 'Alloa', the 4mm OO-gauge layout built by the Scottish Study Group, depicting the ex-North British station in the early 1960s. The signalbox at Alloa Central Junction is the NBR Type 2a, an unusual design because of its smaller windows with brick piers between them. Tony Wright, courtesy of British Railway Modelling

CHAPTER

Modelling the signalbox

Although this signalbox is Magdalen Road near King's Lynn, photographed in 1985, it is not a GER box as you might expect. It is in fact a Great Central Type 5 box, moved here from an unknown location in 1927. The Type 5 was the GCR's last design of box, and more than 100 were built between 1899 and 1930. Magdalen Road station was returned to its original name of Watlington in 1989, but the box was not renamed. *Author*

This chapter is divided into two halves. The first part deals simply with the signalbox model you place on your layout. The second part examines the practical issues to be tackled when making a miniature signalbox from which to operate the railway.

Available buildings

Looking through modelling magazines and online catalogues, you will find that there are numerous examples of signalboxes that can be purchased, some as kits and some ready-made. I thought it would be worthwhile to analyse the available buildings to see just how useful they are. Just as in the fields of locomotives and rolling stock, the GWR modeller is most fortunate. To appreciate all the various types of signalbox I will be mentioning, I would strongly recommend reading *The Signal Box* by the Signalling Study Group (see the Bibliography).

The first signalboxes that the modeller may be aware of, certainly the younger or first-time modeller, are those made by Hornby and Peco, but it is worth looking for types that would better suit your preferences, listed in Table 14.

Table 14: Available signalboxes

Manufacturer and name	Scale	Notes	Company or Region
Hornby			
Signal Box	4mm	Freelance	Any
Thomas Box 1	4mm	Freelance	Any
Thomas Box 2	4mm	Freelance	Any
Magna Box	4mm	Based on MR Type 1, but with brick base and single-finial hipped roof	Any

Skaledale No 4	4mm	GWR Type 4; a good representation of this widespread box, used 1876-1922	GWR and BR (WR)
Lower Skaledale	4mm	Platform box based on Railway Signal Co standard components	Any
Skaledale Junction	4mm	NER Type S1b small box, used in southern area of old NER (Yorkshire)	LNER and BR (NER)
Level Crossing Box	4mm	Small 10-foot-panel MR Type 3a signalbox, without lower storey	LMS and BR (LMR)
Skaledale East	4mm	20-foot MR Type 2a box, although window detail is simplified	LMS and BR (LMR)
Lyddle End Sg Box	2mm	GWR Type 4 (see above)	GWR and BR (WR)
Lyddle End Platform Box	2mm	Platform box (see above)	Any MR
Lyddle End Level Crossing Box	2mm	Type 3a (see above)	LMS and BR (LMR)
Lyddle End Low Level Box	2mm	NER Type	
S1b (see above)		LNER and BR (NER)	LNER and BR
Lyddle End East	2mm	MR Type 2a (see above)	(NER)

Peco

Red Brick Box	4mm/ 2mm	GWR Type 8; good but simplified model of type of box built in 1921-33 period	GWR and BR (WR)
Panel Box	4mm/ 2mm	Good representation of type of modern panel box used by BR (ER) in 1950s, such as Potters Bar	BR (ER)

Bachmann (4mm) and Graham Farish (2mm)

GWR Type 4	4mm/ 2mm	GWR Type 4 box at Highley on Severn Valley Railway	GWR and BR (WR)
Hampton Hill	4mm/ 2mm	Modern-style LNER Type 15 box built from 1944	LNER, BR (ER) and BR (ScR)
Hampton North	4mm/ 2mm	Freelance design reminiscent of Great Central Type 5 box	LNER and BR (ER)
Brick Signal Box	4mm/ 2mm	Very similar to GNR Type 1b boxes of various kinds, particularly East Lincolnshire variety.	LNER and BR (ER)

Dapol

Signal Box	4mm	Very loosely based on MR Type 2b box at Oakham	LMS and BR (LMR)

Ratio

MR Signal Box	4mm/ 2mm	20-foot Midland Type 4 box, as built from 1906 onwards	LMS and BR (LMR)
GW Signal Box	4mm/ 2mm	McKenzie & Holland Type 3 box as used between 1876 and 1922 on several railways, mostly on GWR and Welsh railways	GWR and BR (WR)
Platform Signalbox	4mm/ 2mm	GWR Type 6 platform box, small version of GWR Type 5 from 1889-1902 period	GWR and BR (WR)

Wills

Timber Signalbox	4mm	GER Type 7 box, with some missing timber details, as used 1886-1922; could also pass as GNR box, or be adapted to make GCR Type 5	LNER and BR (ER)
Ground Level Signalbox	4mm	Universal type of ground frame hut that could be successfully used in any location	Any

Knightwing

Signalbox	4mm	Good representation of GNR Type 1a/Arlesey design, built 1874-76	LNER and BR (ER)

Churchward (Modelex)

MR Signalbox	4mm/ 7mm	20-foot Midland Type 4 signalbox	LMS and BR (LMR)
GWR Signalbox	4mm/ 7mm	GWR Type 27 (hipped) timber box as used 1896-1927	GWR and BR (WR)
GWR Signalbox (gabled)	4mm/ 7mm	GWR Type 28c timber box with finials designed c1900 but mostly used from 1921 onwards	GWR and BR, (WR)
LSWR Signalbox	4mm/ 7mm	LSWR Type 3c box as built 1892-95, based on box at Swanage	SR and BR (SR)
LNWR Signalbox	4mm/ 7mm	LNWR Type 4 box as used 1876-1904, very widespread on LNWR system	LMS and BR (LMR)
McKenzie & Holland Signalbox	4mm/ 7mm	Timber version of McKenzie & Holland Type 3 as used between 1876 and 1922 and seen on several railways, mostly GWR and Welsh railways	GWR and BR (WR)

Kestrel

Signalbox	2mm	Freelance, vaguely North London Railway	Any

Metcalfe

Mainline Signalbox	4mm	Freelance, vaguely Saxby & Farmer Type 12	Any

Superquick

Signalbox	4mm/ 2mm	Freelance	Any

P. & D. Marsh

Signalbox	2mm	Freelance	Any

Elro

SER Timber Box	7mm	Timber SER-type box as used 1884-99	SR and BR (SR)

Skytrex

MR Signalbox	7mm	MR Type 2b timber box	MR, M&GN, LMS and BR (LMR)
GWR Ground Frame hut	7mm	Standard GWR hut	GWR and BR (WR)
LNWR Ground Frame hut	7mm	Standard LNWR hut	

This is the Cheshire Lines Committee Type 1a signalbox at Throstle Nest East Junction just west of Manchester in April 1969, one month before it closed. This distinctive and very standardised type of box was used by the CLC from the 1870s to 1903. S. C. Dent

Spondon Station signalbox, built by the Midland in 1918 to its Type 4d design, has the old traditional windows but a brick base. The Ratio and Churchward signalboxes could be adapted to make this box, seen here in 1986. Author

Where the signalbox model is specific to a certain company, there is little that needs to be done other to ensure that the correct colours are used when painting it. The freelance models are not out of the question either, as long as the right colours for your railway company or BR Region are imposed, together with other details such as the right shape of telegraph board. The danger here is that your railway starts to look like everyone else's, so you could adapt and change. Altering the glazing bars in the windows is one example, or turning the stairs through 90 degrees.

'Kit bashing' is a favourite pastime of the British railway modeller, and it's true that plastic kits, such as the Wills signalbox, could easily be adapted. However, that kit suffers in being very railway-specific, although to be a true Great Eastern box, extra timbering has to be added under the operating floor windows. The box could be seen as a Great Northern Type 2, although the arrangement of the upper and lower floor timbering is different, and by adding different designs of bargeboard the modeller could pass this off as a Great Central Type 5 box and even an M&GN box. Claims in the instructions that this type of box could be seen up and down the

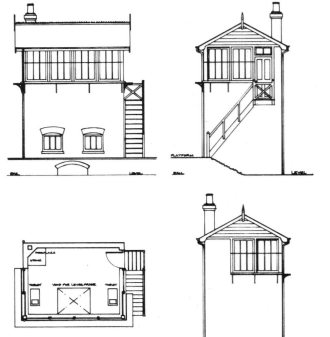

WILKINSON & JARVIS
SIGNAL BOX TYPE 1
AS ERECTED AT
WHITWELL & REEPHAM STATION
AND DRAYTON STATION 1882
NIGEL J. L. DIGBY 1997

Above left: The GER Type 7 signalbox at Cantley was photographed in about 1989. This is the type of box upon which the Wills kit is based. As well as being unusually low, the vertical timber members under the windows are absent, possibly the result of some rebuilding. Author

Above: Canning Street North, seen here in 1981, was an LNWR Type 4 box situated in the midst of the maze of lines that connected with the Birkenhead dock tramways. It is a small version of the type of LNWR box produced by Churchward. Author

Left: A drawing of the Wilkinson & Jarvis signalboxes erected at Whitwell & Reepham and Drayton stations. Author

Below: A model in 4mm scale of the Saxby & Farmer Type 5 box at Eridge, in BR (SR) colours. Author

This is a 4mm model of a Caledonian Type S4 signalbox, a design that was used on the Southern Division of the Caley from 1870 right up to the Grouping. Author

country simply do not hold water, and the suggestion that this is a Saxby & Farmer-type box is incorrect; the company did build some like this, but from GER drawings. Strangely, by adding the appropriate bargeboards and finials, and removing the lower horizontal glazing bars from the operating floor windows, the box is quite a successful representation of the type erected by Evans, O'Donnell for the South Eastern Railway.

The Ratio Midland box is the MR Type 4a, built 1906-17. The length is 20 feet, made up of two standard 10-foot panels. These were built in the signal works at Derby, and assembled on site. By replacing the lower storey at the front with plain panels, a Type 2b box of 1894-1906 could be simulated, although the boarding should be weatherboarding, not the lapped boarding on the model. Careful scraping with a scalpel would serve to make the slight backward slope of weatherboarding. The Type 2b was more numerous, and had a few examples on the M&GN. The roof sits a little too high on the model because the facia board on which the guttering is fixed has been moulded as solid, rather than allowing the panels to rise behind it. This can be trimmed away to bring the roof down.

Signalbox size

The size of a signalbox is directly related to the number of levers in the lever frame – it would be inappropriate to supply a large box at a small location. Gatewheels or tablet instruments may require space at the side of the frame, but it should be quite easy, after designing the signalling, to work out the length of box needed – it will probably be less than you expect. The Midland in particular was a small box line. By careful cutting of the Ratio kit, a 30-foot version could be made from two kits (three 10-foot panels), but your station would have to be very large indeed to justify it.

Scratch-building

If the kits or ready-built signalboxes are not appropriate to your prototype, there is only one alternative – build one. A professional modelmaker could be engaged, but many people do not have the funds for such a project, so modellers must build it themselves 'from scratch'. A possible alternative, if they are handy with a drawing pen or Computer Aided Design (CAD), is to have an etched brass kit made;

Scratch-building 1: The initial carcass of a 7mm GER Type 7 box built for Major Henry King. The lines for applying the boarding were drawn on the card before assembly. Author

Scratch-building 2: The rear of the finished signalbox, showing the boarding, the ventilator and the stovepipe. Author

Scratch-building 3: The front of the finished signalbox, showing the stairs, fire buckets and how important it is that the interior is modelled. Note the open window and door, a typical occurrence in summer. Author

Scratch-building 4: The interior has a 25-lever frame, the base of which can be seen through the locking room windows, and two tablet machines for single-line working. Author

there are several firms prepared to do one-off etches for modellers, and it may take the drudgery out of scribing planking or cutting out window frames. Nevertheless, there is something satisfying about taking some sheets of card and plastic and transforming them into a recognisable building.

This is not the place to discuss building methods. Suffice it to say that there are many resources available to the scratch-builder, including embossed plastic sheeting, etched brass or plastic windows, plastic and metal sections, cast metal gutters and downpipes, and many other items designed to make the construction of your own buildings easier and more realistic.

A reliable and accurate drawing is essential to make your signalbox. This could be found in books on the subject (see *The Signal Box*) or more possibly in the archives of the relevant line society. Failing this, a surviving example could be measured and photographed, having first obtained permission.

Signalbox colours

It is vital to paint your signalbox in the correct colours for company and period, and Table 15 provides a simple list of the kind of colours you will need. The usual scheme on railways was to paint the larger area of a signalbox such as planking a light colour (almost invariably cream), and contrast it with corner posts, framing, steps and so on in a darker colour – very often a brown. The cream was not normally the pale colour we think of now, but more of a buff colour with distinct yellow and even pink overtones. This might be referred to as 'stone' in the companies' records, and the contrast colour on the GWR was 'dark stone'. However 'dark stone' on the Southern was a cream!

Window glazing bars were white, unless otherwise specified, and metal items such as stovepipes, walkway brackets and walkway safety rails were usually black. Nameboards were often black letters on a white background or vice versa, but sometimes enamel plates of various colours.

Table 15: Signalbox colours

GWR	'Light stone' and 'dark stone'
BR (WR)	BR cream (biscuit) and golden brown
Cambrian	Cream and green
TVR	Buff
B&M	Salmon brown and black
M&SWJ	Buff and brown
LNER	Stone and brown until 1937, when stone and green was introduced
BR (ER)	BR cream (biscuit) and green
BR (NER)	Ivory (light grey) and Oriental Blue (sky blue)
NER	Buff, including glazing bars, and red-brown
GNR	Light stone and dark stone; glazing bars light green; timber boxes painted dark brown up to 4 feet above ground level, where there was a 1½-inch black band
GER	Stone and brown oxide (reddish brown)
GCR	Cream and light brown, with lower part of timber boxes painted red-brown; from 1912 light green and dark green
M&GN	Stone and tan
H&B	Cream and brown
LMS	Until 1931, as for pre-Grouping company; from 1931 stone and red brown, with some stone and green c1936
BR (LMR)	BR cream (biscuit) and maroon
MR	Lemon chrome and Venetian red; blue background to nameboard
LNWR	Stone and light brown
L&Y	Tan and brown
FR	Cream and madder lake (red-brown)
NSR	Cream and purple brown up to 1900, thereafter cream and Indian red
LT&SR	Cream and green
SR	'Dark stone' and 'middle chrome green'
BR (SR)	BR cream (biscuit) and middle chrome green
LSWR	Salmon and dark brown
LBSCR	Cream (including glazing bars) and dark red
SECR	Buff and red brown
S&D	Buff and brown
BR (ScR)	BR cream (biscuit) and brown
CR	Cinnamon and purple brown
HR	Burnt sienna and purple brown; corrugated-iron roofs red oxide
NBR	Cream and brown or light green and dark green
G&SW	Reddish brown, dark brown for gutters and downpipes; corrugated-iron roofs red oxide
GNoS	Cream and brown

Interiors

To finish the signalbox, it is a good idea to be able to see some internal details, particularly as the windows are usually quite large. The most obvious features are the levers and the block shelf over them supporting the instruments. Then there may be single-line token machines to consider, and possibly a gatewheel as well. All these can be made from simple materials; for example, I have read of a lever frame being made from a plastic hair comb. Scraps of card and plastic are enough to suggest the other equipment. Look at photos of signalbox interiors for inspiration. However, there are kits for box interiors, those produced by Wills and Ratio being well known.

The interior walls on the operating floor of a typical box were painted brown (or possibly green) up to dado level – about waist height – then cream or white above. The floor was a light brown lino, or bare wood. The quadrants of the lever frame were black, as was the stove or cast-iron fireplace. Levers were painted red, black, blue, brown, green or yellow according to their function (see Chapter 3), with polished metal handles. The instruments and tablet machines were usually in cases of varnished wood, and block bells were polished brass. The signalling diagram was hung over the block shelf.

After having gone to the trouble of detailing the interior, a nice touch is to light it. A white grain of wheat bulb or LED (light-emitting diode) can be given a paper lampshade and suspended from the roof, or mounted on the back wall by the desk like an oil lamp. Only a low light level is needed, so make sure the current going to the bulb is very small, which also makes it last longer. It might be as well to make the roof demountable so that you can replace bulbs or make other alterations once the model is finished.

The working signalbox

Drawing all the separate threads together, you can now design a signalbox from which to actually work your layout. The position of the box on the baseboard ought to be near the actual model of the signalbox, but this is not always possible. I always design my stations to be 'two-handers', in other words with a driver/shunter and a signalman working as a team. The placing of the equipment therefore has to take account of where the two operators can stand or sit.

The type of operating box you decide to build may be determined by where it can be put on the baseboard, and the method of point and signal control. On my layout 'White Swan' I was fortunate in that buildings could be used to conceal the box, and I was able to simply mount it on the board and use wire-in-tube control for many of the points, and cord and pulleys for the signals. You may prefer to use electric motors, and on 'East Walsham', which is both an exhibition layout designed to be worked from behind the backscene, and a home layout to be worked from the front, I cannot do anything else. In this case, a separate structure can be clipped or bolted onto the baseboard, and the necessary wires then connected with multi-pin plugs. My ultimate aim is to have a $\frac{1}{2}$th-scale model of the actual 'East Walsham' signalbox, mounted on a free-standing trolley with all the proper equipment inside. This would be as near to the experience of being a real signalman on the railway as I could manage.

At the heart of the box is, of course, the lever frame. There are only two manufacturers of miniature mechanical working frames to choose from, Modratec in Australia, and Model Signal Engineering. Both are excellent in their own way, particularly the Modratec system, where the locking is worked out for you, but of course both have cost implications. For the more cost-conscious, it isn't difficult to fabricate a lever frame from metal sheet for the quadrant guides, with metal bar for the levers. In the past I have reused some old GEM frames my father had, and where I needed more levers I copied their construction. The GEM frames are still available from Model Signal Engineering and have the virtue of being very simple. For those wanting a larger and more realistic frame, Scale Signal Supply makes a

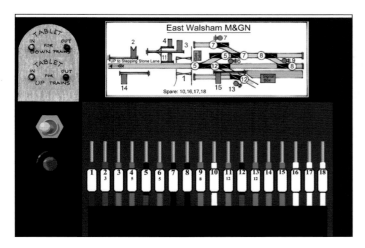

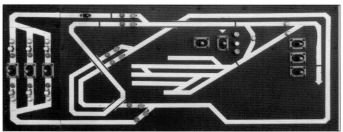

The working model railway signalbox: a plan for the projected signalbox at East Walsham.

Perhaps the more usual method of control used by modellers, the panel. This was my father's layout in the 1970s. Can you guess the M&GN location? Author

½th-scale kit of the Stevens lever frame. I think I will have to have that for my ½th scale 'East Walsham' signalbox one day.

For electrical operation, the problem is that solenoid-type point motors (see below) require a 'passing contact' switch to prevent them burning out. In other words, only a single burst of current is needed rather than a continuous connection, usually 16v AC, taken from the rear of traditional controllers or transformers provided specially for the task. The only manufacturers of passing contact switches that look like signalbox levers are Hornby and Peco, and these can be assembled in a line like a lever frame. Don't forget to paint the levers the correct colours, and to mount lever numbers on them. Another method is to use a 'push to make' button. The levers are then simply a directional switch, so can be standard DPDT toggle switches. The push button mounted below sends the pulse of current.

An alternative to the mechanical lever frame is to reproduce a 'panel', where thumb or radio switches show the direction of points, or the status of signals. Unless passing-contact switches of this kind can be purchased, or home-made, this type of operation suggests the 'tortoise' type of point motor. A variation would be to use push buttons instead, and of course many modellers use the 'electric pencil' approach. This is probably the simplest method of electrical point control, where the wires controlling the point motors are soldered to bolts or paper clips mounted on a panel, and the activating current is supplied by a floating wire, touching each point as required. The disadvantage of these switching methods is that interlocking, at least in the mechanical sense, cannot be incorporated.

Although my ultimate aim is more sophisticated, in the short term I will be using my standard method of simulating a signalbox. This is to surround the lever frame with a fascia, simply cut from plywood and stained a darker colour. Above the levers, allowing enough space for fingers, is the signalling diagram. To the left is a representation of the tablet instrument, with its green face and tablet IN/OUT indicator replaced by coloured lights. The gong and its activating solenoid are mounted behind the fascia under the baseboard. On double lines, the combined block instruments are represented instead of the tablet machines.

A through station or a junction, such as Stepping Stone Lane Junction box, will be more complicated, with block instruments or tablet machines controlling the line from each end, but as presently intended one tablet instrument is all that will be required for East Walsham. Further development of the layout after it is built will demand a second machine, but that is looking far ahead.

The locking frame

Below the levers will be the locking tray. Probably the easiest way to construct this, although not necessarily the most economical, is to make up a tray of brass sheet with slots at top and bottom to guide the tappets. In the tray, strips of 5mm by 60 thou brass are soldered to form channels in which locking bars of the same brass strip can slide, arranged across the tray in a grid, locking bars under tappets. Locks are made up from pieces of the same strip filed to shape and soldered to their locking bars, and ports are simply filed out of the tappets in the appropriate places.

To combine several locking bars in one channel, the locks slide on as small a piece of bar as possible, and are joined to their fellows by thin-section rod, soldered on the front face, up to three side by side.

The tray is mounted below, in front or behind the lever frame, and the tappets connected to each lever by a sturdy linkage, such as piano wire. The precise dimensions can be adjusted according to the frame used and the throw given by the levers, but I have assumed a 5mm spacing and 5mm throw, merely for the sake of illustration. Having the throw the same dimension as the separation of the bars avoids conflicts with perhaps the wrong lock going into the wrong port. The number of locking bars needed and the types of lock can be worked out before construction by drawing out a locking chart as detailed in Chapters 5 and 6.

Point control

For point motors I still have a stock of old H&M solenoid types, although their on-board switches can become unreliable after a time. These are now unobtainable except on sites like eBay. There are several alternatives of the solenoid type. The SEEP motor has versions with and without switching. The switching is used to change the polarity of the crossing, indispensable if you have hand-made points such as C&L or if you have soldered construction from rail and copperclad sleepers. Peco and Hornby have solenoid motors, but as their turnouts don't need switching (it is incorporated in the design of the point), their motors are not fitted with it. Peco make a subsidiary switch that can be added to the assembly. MSE makes a latching solenoid for point or signal control.

The other type of point motor is the 'slow-action' sort, which uses a rotating armature like a regular locomotive motor. A continuous current is supplied until the motor reaches the end of its travel when it stalls and stops. Fulgarex, Tortoise and Conrad manufacture this type of motor.

The motors themselves can be mounted either on top of or below the baseboard. Being on top is certainly convenient, and a wire (incorporating an 'omega' loop to allow a slightly variable length of throw) can be installed directly between the motor and the point. Small lineside huts are sold to cover motors like this, and bushes or the topography can also conceal them. However, if the workings necessary for point control are to be concealed more effectively, then under the baseboard is best.

There is always a tension here between the practical, where a sturdy linkage between the switch rails is needed to withstand the rigours of constant activation, and the prototype, where the stretcher bars are actually very slender. Most modellers have to be content with a 'moveable sleeper' approach, where the switch rails are soldered or riveted to a crosspiece that resembles another sleeper. It may also have the switching for the crossing mounted on it. It is possible to conceal this sleeper under the trackbed with stiff vertical wires making contact with the switch rails. The method I have used on 'East Walsham' is to combine the C&L insulated stretcher bars with a piece of copperclad sleeper for strength, and a wire loop. The stretcher bar is moved by a rigid rod engaging with the loop, and passing through the baseboard to be soldered into a piece of brass bar sliding in a section of curtain rail. The point motor is nearby, attached to the brass bar with piano wire having an omega loop to allow flexing.

Modelling block instruments

The full-size instruments used relays and various other means to keep the number of wires between signalboxes to a minimum. On a model there is no such restriction, so a working representation of block instruments can easily be achieved. By the use of three-position switches for double line, and two-position switches for single line, it can be arranged to have coloured lights (grain of wheat bulbs or LEDs) to show the Line Blocked/Line Clear/Train on Line indications, or tablet IN/OUT. The diagram shows the method I use, with two power sources; 4v DC for the lights and 11v AC for the bells, which have redundant point motor coils to activate the striker. For bells I used children's bicycle bells, and for gongs I used a square cigar tin base, which makes a nice clanging sound. The block bells were 'tuned' by sawing off a portion of one to make its tone higher.

In my previous layouts, the tablet and double-line instruments I made were not actually separate. I incorporated them into the plywood fascia surrounding the lever frames, with the signalling diagram glued above the levers. Holes were drilled in the fascia to accept the bulbs, switches and bell pushes required.

The process of operating a double line remains precisely as described in Chapter 3, with white, green and red bulbs or LEDs for the three block settings rather than needles, but single-line working needs a little simplification, as there are no commutators, or tablets for that matter. It is worked similarly to the double line, but in reverse, as it is the home signalman who changes the switch (withdraws a tablet) rather than the remote signalman giving Line Clear. When a train is to be sent, the appropriate code is rung. If permission is given by acknowledging the signal, the sending signalman changes his switch to Tablet Out, which is effectively withdrawing a tablet. The instrument in the receiving box also now shows Tablet Out (a red light). Train Entering Section is sent and acknowledged as usual. On arrival of the train, the receiving signalman sends Train Out of Section, confirming in effect that he has put the tablet into his instrument. The sending box then acknowledges Train Out of Section and returns his switch to the normal Tablet In. The instrument is now returned to normal. Several steps have been omitted but the overall effect is the same.

A working combined block instrument ready for use at Stepping Stone Lane Junction. Author

A locking frame built from steel channel and brass bar by Mick Nicholson. The tappets are connected to the levers, with the locking bars crossing them in horizontal channels.
Mick Nicholson

The wiring diagram for a pair of tablet machines at each end of a modelled single-line section. Author

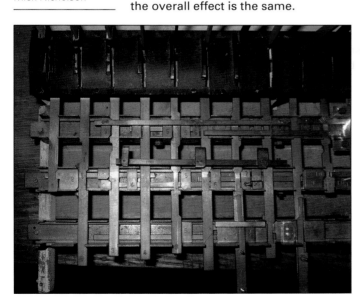

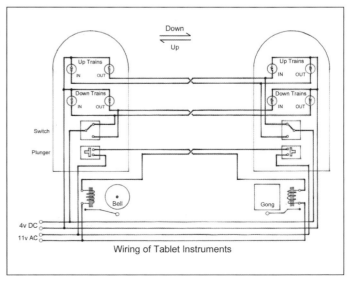

Wiring of Tablet Instruments

Modelling the signals

Caledonian lower-quadrant signals. The left-hand doll has a miniature semaphore used for goods or slow-line movements. The lattice posts and finials are almost certainly a Stevens product. The balance lever pivot castings carry the word CALEDONIAN curved around the bearing. Ian Allan Library

Company variety

In the earliest days of the railways, a number of unusual designs of signal evolved. However, by the time period covered by this book (from 1890) signalling had become standardised, although the individuals in charge of the signalling departments of the railway companies still managed to create their own variations as unique to each railway as its locomotives, rolling stock, signalboxes or any other aspect the company's 'house style'.

The signalling contractors were the early drivers of the evolution of the railway semaphore, and some railways took on aspects of contractors' designs and perpetuated them as their own once they had established signal works, which most of them did in the 1870s and '80s. The early work of Stevens and Saxby &

Farmer can be traced in these signals. Sometimes this process worked in the other direction. McKenzie & Holland did a lot of work for the GNR, and seems to have formed a favourable opinion of that company's somersault signals, because for its subsequent work in Wales for the Taff Vale and Rhymney railways, and also elsewhere in the world, McKenzie & Holland used just that design.

Another area that could indicate the likely source of a signal design was the post. The contractor Stevens favoured the lattice iron post, and since Stevens supplied signalling equipment to all the Scottish railways except the Highland, lattice posts were almost ubiquitous north of the border. Lattice posts could be seen elsewhere, on the LSWR for example, but timber was the normal material for signal posts on most other railways until the Grouping, when steel (round section or fabricated from angle and plate) replaced it. The Southern Railway cleverly used redundant bullhead rail. Generally speaking the semaphore arms were mounted in front of the posts, sometimes pivoted through the post, sometimes with the pivot on a casting beside the post, as on the LNWR and GWR. The North Eastern had a different approach from other railways, as it still mounted its semaphores inside slotted posts when all other British railways had abandoned them.

The drawback of using timber for signal posts was that they had to be planed to a taper, they had to be painted, and they had a tendency to decay. Concrete avoided all of these problems. From around 1914, several companies experimented with reinforced concrete for signal posts, but the only successful design was that developed by William Marriott of the M&GN. This was manufactured under licence by Ellis & Sons of Leicester, and during the 1920s and '30s many concrete posts were erected on the LNER and M&GN, and a few on the MR/LMS, some still surviving in use today.

Finials were another indicator of company ownership. Although most were based on the 'ball and spike', the myriad ways they were executed was astonishing. Some were made of turned wood, others from iron strip with spaces between, and others of cast iron. The ball and spike finials on the M&GN were fabricated from zinc and, while being similar to GNR finials, differed from them in having the base of the spike six-sided, forming a hexagon in plan. The spikes could be short or anything up to 3 feet long. Among the most decorative finials were those used by McKenzie & Holland, which had a very long spike and an umbrella

Below: *LBSCR signals at Sheffield Park in the 1950s. The fixings for the spectacle plate were adjustable to allow for different widths of post.*
The miniature arm, although an original LBSCR lower-quadrant, has been painted with a horizontal white stripe and fitted with an S for 'Shunt' by the Southern Railway. B. Nunns/ A. Mott collection

Centre: *These GER signals at Cromer High station are seen in 1952, just before their replacement by the BR (ER) bracket post being erected behind them. The signals are on the right-hand side of the line for sighting purposes. Note two McKenzie & Holland finials, and two later standard GER cast-iron caps. The GER favoured very tall posts, and here the main Stop signals have co-acting repeaters mounted on the lower part of the post.* W. S. Garth

Left: *A South Eastern & Chatham goods signal guarding the exit from the goods yard at Westerham, terminus of the former SER branch from Dunton Green, still in situ in 1961.* J. Scrace

Superb GER signals on 'East Lynn', the S-gauge layout by Trevor Nunn, set in west Norfolk in 1903. The Calling-on signals are prominent. Tony Wright, courtesy of British Railway Modelling

The upper Stop arm of this Midland Railway signal is corrugated steel, and the lower Distant is wooden. The unusual shape of the spectacles, introduced circa 1900, is apparent. The D-shaped loops rising diagonally from the arm spindles were to prevent the arm from rising above the horizontal. Malcolm Cross

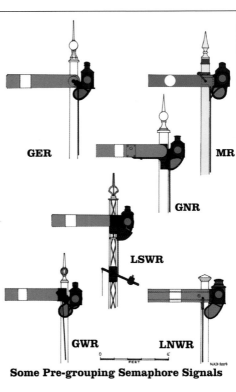

A selection of pre-Grouping semaphore signals. Author

Some Pre-grouping Semaphore Signals

shape rather than a ball. Possibly the most consistent company was the Midland, whose distinctive finial was turned from pitch pine.

Painting of the signals varied between companies, too. Although white (for visibility) was the majority choice for signal posts, not all companies used it; until about 1906 the Midland painted its posts the same lemon chrome that distinguished its signalboxes. The lower 5 feet of signal posts and ironwork such as ladders, brackets and balance weights were usually painted black, but again several railways used brown for these areas, notably the LNWR and the MR. The signal arms themselves also showed differences. The Midland, the SER and the

Cambrian all shared the use of a white spot or roundel on the red of the arms, although the MR changed its policy from about 1906 and began to use the standard white stripe. Even the position of the white stripes varied, the LNWR among others setting them quite far away from the tips of the arms, while early GNR somersault signals actually had them halfway along at the pivot. The Welsh lines using somersault arms had two stripes per arm, one at each end.

On the rear face of its Distant arms, until about 1911 the MR used a black horizontal stripe. The reading faces of Distant arms were also subject to variation, the chevron following the 'fishtail' cut-out by no means being universal. The LNWR, MR, GNR, NBR, WR, NER and FR all used a plain white stripe. It was not until after 1925 that the yellow Distant arm with black chevron became commonplace, and even then there was some resistance. Numerous enamelled yellow somersault arms on the ex-GNR lines and the M&GN were installed still with a plain black stripe.

Available signals

Considering their importance, the number of semaphore signals available straight from the box is very small. The problem is of course that signals were tailored to suit their situation; their height and the positioning of extra arms would vary according to the layout of the location. On the prototype, when signals were being installed a committee of officers from the various departments would visit the site and determine all the visibility factors before deciding on the length of post and disposition of arms.

This variability of all but the simplest signals certainly makes the provision of ready-made examples more difficult. The Hornby junction bracket signal, for example, presupposes that your secondary line diverges to the left, and that company's choice to market a splitting Distant signal is unfortunate because, as we have seen, Distant signals rarely feature on layouts due to lack of space. Moreover, in the era that the signal post is designed to represent, a single Distant would suffice. In short, the modeller really only has one recourse – build from a kit, or build from scratch. Ready-made and kit signals are listed in Table 16.

The LSWR was a user of lattice signal posts, thanks to their use of Stevens as signalling contractor. The starting signals on 'Rothern Bridge' show the LSWR design – this 7mm O-gauge layout was based on Torrington in Devon, and was constructed by the Crawley Model Railway Society. Tony Wright, British Railway Modelling

Table 16: Semaphore signals

UQ = upper-quadrant; LQ = lower-quadrant

Manufacturer	Scale	Type
Hornby	4mm	Lattice-post UQ Home, Distant, Junction Home, Junction Distant
Ratio	4mm/ some 2mm	GWR LQ square-post Home, Home and Distant, Distant, Bracket/Junction GWR LQ round-post Home, Home and Distant, Distant, bracket/junction LMS UQ round-post Home, Home and Distant, Distant, bracket/junction LNER UQ round-post Home, Home and Distant, Distant, bracket/junction LNER UQ lattice-post Home, Home and Distant, Distant, bracket/junction SR UQ rail-built-post Home, Home and Distant, Distant LNWR LQ square-post Home, Home and Distant, Distant, bracket/junction Ground signals (BR type) Pratt truss gantry
Model Signal Engineering (MSE)	4mm some 2mm 7mm 10mm	Signal arms, ground signals, lamps and finials for most pre-Grouping and Grouping companies; lattice, timber and concrete posts, lattice gantries, ladders, brackets and spectacle glazing
P. & D. Marsh	2mm some 4mm	GWR LQ timber-post Home, Home and Distant, Home bracket, junction bracket, triple bracket, gantry GWR LQ round-post Home, Home and Distant, Home bracket, junction bracket, four-doll bracket LMS UQ lattice-post Home, Home and Distant, Home bracket, junction bracket, triple bracket, gantry
Scale Signal Supply	7mm	LNWR Home, junction, ground signal GWR Home, Distant, junction, route indicators, ground signal. GNR Home, Distant, timber posts and lattice MR Home, Distant, junction, ground signal GER Home, Distant NER slotted-post Home, Distant, junction L&Y Home, Distant LBSCR Home, Distant SR UQ Home, Distant, junction, ground signal, rail and lattice posts LMS/BR UQ Home, Distant, junction, miniature, ground signal, wood and lattice posts LNER/BR UQ Home, Distant, junction, miniature, ground signal, wood and lattice posts

Users of colour-light signals fare much better, as there are a variety of two-, three- and four-aspect signals available for use straight out of the box (see Table 17). The use of LEDs in most examples ensures that these signals are not unprototypically deep.

Table 17: Colour-light signals

Manufacturer	Scale	Type
Train Tronics	2mm/4mm	Two-, three- and four-aspect, with junction indicators
Berko	4mm	Two-, three- and four-aspect, with junction pairs and offset posts
Eckon Kits	4mm	Two-, three- and four-aspect, with junction pairs and junction indicators, ground signals
Hornby	4mm	Two-aspect

Kits and scratch-building

This is not a treatise on signal-building per se; for that I would direct you to Mick Nicholson's excellent work. However, the provision of a myriad of etched signal arms, fittings, posts and other items from MSE ensures that, with the dedication of a little time, almost any conceivable signal is within the reach of the average modeller. Those with less time may be able to take advantage of the Ratio plastic kits, particularly if they are modelling the Grouping period.

The first requirement before making a model of a signal is a photograph. The photo may not be precisely of the actual signal, since you may have difficulty finding one, or your layout may be fictional, but a signal of the right general type can usually be found. This is where extensive reading or collecting of magazine articles is invaluable. A line drawing is also indispensable, but if one is unavailable, a drawing, or at least a dimensioned sketch, can be made from a photograph by remembering that the standard semaphore arm was usually 5 feet long from tip to spindle. Many signalling books contain 'typical' drawings that can be used to understand details not obvious from photos.

The first stage is to make up the signal post. Posts are available in white metal and other materials generally up to a scale length of 25 feet, which is a little short in my opinion. I would say the average pre-Grouping signal arm was at least 30 feet above rail level. However, it is not hard to make posts to suit your own needs. When I need to make them, I obtain 5mm or 6mm square-section spruce and fit it into a jig. This is simply some small-section stripwood mounted on a base to form a slot for the post, with a stop at the top to prevent the post moving forward. Clamp the jig to the bench, take a small woodworking plane set to a very fine shave, and

Signals were tailored to suit their situation: the impressive gantry of LNWR signals at Rugby was outlined against the sky above the GCR girder bridge, and repeated by co-acting lower arms nearer the drivers' eye level.
Ian Allan Library

A Model Signal Engineering kit for a Midland signal. Author

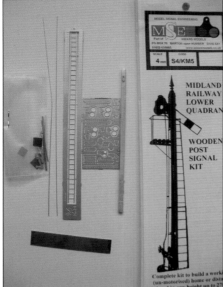

A Model Signal Engineering kit for a Midland signal. Author

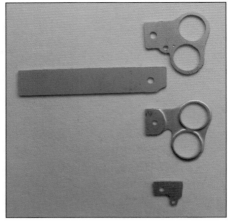

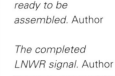

The MSE etched components to make the Midland signal arm. Author

The components of a two-arm LNWR signal painted and ready to be assembled. Author

The completed LNWR signal. Author

The contents of the Ratio LNWR signal kit. Generous provision of mouldings enables the construction of several signals. Author

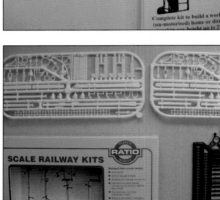

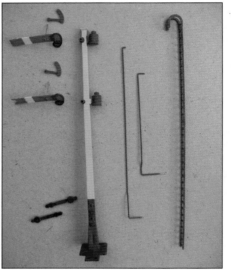

take one shave at a time from each side, turning the post between strokes and always working towards the top. In no time a tapered post will result. Batch-make several at once. Some can be planed to a more slender section to be used as dolls on bracket posts. A quick rub with fine glasspaper will remove any rough areas, then lightly dress off the corners; timber posts invariably had a chamfer at each corner. A similar process can be followed with square-section brass, using a file.

It depends very much on your operating method how your signal post is fitted to the layout, particularly if the layout is portable and the signals are required to be removed from the baseboard. The usual method is to employ a baseplate on which to assemble the signal, located at the site by lugs, pins or screws into the baseboard, and the operating wires coming up from below.

Modern tubular steel posts are a simple marriage of two sizes of brass tube, with the main post of 1/16-inch diameter tube and the 'butt' or thicker lower part of 3/32-inch diameter. The height of a tubular post signal from rail to arm was standardised at 16ft, 20ft, 22ft 6in, 25ft, 27ft 6in and 30ft. For the first two sizes, a butt of 6 feet above rail level was used, with 10 feet for the rest.

Lattice posts are a little more fiddly to make from the MSE range, but as long as a good steel straight-edge is used to make a sharp bend in the two halves of the etch they can be soldered together with no trouble.

Brackets for junction signals, or subsidiary signals attached to the main posts, whatever their construction, are easily obtained in cast metal or etched brass, or can be cut out of Plasticard. The more elaborate cast-iron spandrels beloved of railways like the GER would have to be an etched product.

Although it may seem a tiny detail, having the correct lamp for your signal is a good way of setting it in time. Before the Grouping there were a variety of designs, some with elaborate chimney cowls, or large cases, usually round. From the 1920s lamps increasingly became standardised as the square-pattern Adlake type. Present-day signals have the strangely shaped electric lamps.

Balance weights are an essential part of the signal's construction. Every operable arm had one, principally to keep the signal wire taut, as the arm and spectacle were self-balancing. In other words, if there was a fault with the linkage, the arm would rise or fall to Danger as the default position. If there was also a Distant signal arm on the post, there would inevitably be slotting, an arrangement of three balance weights (see Chapter 4).

The signal arm appropriate to the modelled company is of course vital. Being made up of separate spectacle plate and arm, they can be fiddly to assemble in the etched brass kits. This is where a plastic kit can win out for simplicity, but unfortunately the spectacle glass is moulded solid, and therefore either has to be cut out (a fiddly job) or painted, losing the transparency of the prototype. I would have thought that arms could be moulded in clear plastic, then dabs of transparent colour as used for glass painting could preserve the appearance of glazing.

The finial completes the signal. All posts were topped with something, even if it was only a cap, such as on tubular posts. Cast white-metal finials for nearly every company are available from MSE. However, for my M&GN finials I had to use the MSE GNR ball and spike, with most of the portion below the ball cut out and the two pieces superglued together to form the correct silhouette. That is typical behaviour for the M&GN modeller, where almost nothing commercially available is suitable for our use, but adherents of more 'mainstream' lines, particularly the GWR, will be luckier in their choice of fittings.

Painting

Before final assembly, the signal needs to be painted. Spraying everything with white primer from motor accessory shops is the usual first step. The appropriate colours can then be brushed on. After the primer, I prefer to brush a pale grey on my signal posts – in fact, on most things that should be white – as pure white can be too glaring at a small scale. Care must of course be taken when painting the signal arms to achieve straight lines; some etches and plastic kits have guiding lines to follow. Spectacle plates and pivot castings were generally black, but not always so. The LNWR carried its brown policy to this area as well, and the spectacle plates on upper-quadrant signals were sometimes the same colour as the arms. The LMS took to painting some of its spectacle plates white, particularly the ex-Midland ones. Leave the fitting of the spectacle glazing until after painting. MSE markets the appropriate colour gels for spectacles, which it must be remembered are ruby, cyan and amber, not red, green and yellow. They are fixed in the etching by gloss varnish, or a smear of gel superglue.

Operation

Just as point operation seems to have as many different methods as there are modellers, signal control can also have many alternatives, often down to personal preference. The simplest is probably a wire-in-tube system, or cord and pulleys. Both MSE and Modratec market a cord system. Of course there is no reason why electric solenoid motors cannot be used, and that is the method I am using on 'East Walsham'. MSE markets both a latching solenoid and a continuous current solenoid, and recently have added the Viessman damped solenoid, which gives a slow actuation. Relays were popular at one time, with extended arms fitted, although they are harder to obtain today. More recently the servo motors as fitted to radio-controlled models have been drafted in. 'The Bouncer' control board controls up to four servos, incorporating the slow pull off and bouncing return of real signals, and is marketed by Full Stop Signals. This is the latest electronic

The Up Home at Leadenham, Lincolnshire. The rear view of this GNR somersault arm shows the actuating rod, the casting on the rear of the arm and the backshade fitted with a purple spectacle glass. The finial has lost its spike. R. O. Tuck

incarnation of something that has exercised many modeller's minds over the years, although signalmen have stated to me that the so-called 'bounce' effect on anything but an upper-quadrant signal is simply the result of sloppy work in the signalbox!

A method of operation gaining popularity in recent years is the use of nitinol or 'memory wire'. This wire has the property of contracting by 5% when subjected to a very small electrical current, returning to its original length with the aid of a light spring when the current is switched off. The amount of shortening is therefore proportional to the length of wire supplied. Its adoption for signalling is an obvious step, where the wire can be connected directly to a crank to amplify the movement, and mounted below the signal under the baseboard.

Where problems may arise is if signals are meant to be demountable, that is to say removable from the baseboard. Many modellers prefer to do this on portable layouts to protect the delicate mechanisms. In this case the signal is mounted with its mechanism and 'plugged in' to a receiving socket on the baseboard. If operated by cord or wire-in-tube, it is a simple matter to attach or detach the linkage. If electrically operated, the motor can actually be attached to

the mounting and only the wires would be unplugged. An alternative would be to have the signal operating wires terminate with weighted droppers, which could be lifted by paddles or flat plates moved by the motor – there would be no physical connection to detach. The MSE signal-operating mechanism, a beautifully engineered etched brass crank system, is also able to detach the pull wire, allowing the whole assembly to be lifted out.

On my previous layout, 'White Swan', the signals were permanently attached, and I used home-made cranks below, fitted with their own balance weights. This returned the signals to danger when the cord and pulley linkage to the lever frame was relaxed by returning the lever to normal.

The actual operating wire on the signal can present problems. It must be strong enough to be pushed without deflecting, but must also be thin enough not to be too obvious. Brass or nickel silver wire of 0.3mm or 0.5mm diameter is suitable. Rod guides, rather like small handrail knobs, keep the rods on the prototype in place up the corner or face of the signal post, but as they are so small it is difficult to model them in the smaller scales. If the signal is a tall one, the thicker wire is probably best.

Once up on the signal, the operating wire may have to reach arms on dolls from brackets or along a gantry. The conventional way to do this would be to fit cranks. A simpler alternative, although not prototypical, is to bend the wire into right-

The same type of signal was installed by McKenzie & Holland on the Taff Vale Railway. The TVR painted the arms with two white stripes, shown here on 'Aberdare', the 4mm OO-gauge layout by the Cardiff 4mm Group. Tony Wright, courtesy of British Railway Modelling

The Cambrian Railways used more conventional lower-quadrant arms, but adopted a white spot, as can be seen on 'Johnstown Road', the 7mm O-gauge layout by the Barrowmore Model Railway Group, set on the Cambrian in 1908. Tony Wright, courtesy of British Railway Modelling

angles to follow the necessary route to the doll or dolls, and the whole wire then moves up and down.

You may think that the balance weight levers are a handy place to join the signal push rod with the operating mechanism below, and in the available ready-made signals or kits that is the method chosen. However, the balance weights look overscale and do not lend themselves to adaptation – to represent a slot for a Distant signal, for example. The places where the wires have to be linked to the balance weight can introduce 'slop' into the operation, too. It is probably better to model the balance weights as dummies, with the actual operating wire passing straight down through the baseboard to the mechanism below. This allows the chain wheel (or possibly wire crank), which brought the pull of the wire from the signalbox to the signal itself, to be modelled and connected to the balance lever.

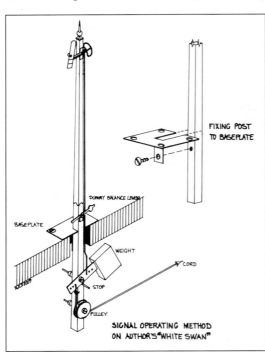

The operating method for signals used by the author on 'White Swan', a 4mm OO-gauge layout.

Bibliography and further reading

Back, Michael *The Signalling of the M&GN* (manuscript)
Beal, Edward *Modelling the Old-Time Railways* (A. & C. Black)
Byles, C. B. *First Principles of Railway Signalling* (Railway Gazette, 1910)
Dow, George and Lacey, R. E. *Midland Style* (HMRS, 1975)
Essery, Bob *Railway Signalling and Track Plans* (Ian Allan, 2007)
Nicholson, Mick *Semaphore Signals* (Booklaw Publications, 1999)
Nock, O. S. *British Railway Signalling* (George Allen & Unwin, 1969)
Pigg, James *Railway Block Signalling* (Biggs & Co, 1898)
Pre-Grouping Atlas and Gazetteer (Ian Allan, 1958/1997)
Signalling Study Group *The Signalbox* (OPC, 1986)
Vanns, Michael A. *Signalling in the Age of Steam* (Ian Allan, 1995)
    An Illustrated History of Signalling (Ian Allan, 1997)
    An Illustrated History of Great Northern Signalling (OPC, 2000)

M&GN Appendix to the Working Timetables, 1913

Useful websites

www.signalbox.org
www.stationcolours.info
www.newrailwaymodellers.co.uk
www.irail.co.uk
www.rmweb.co.uk
www.old-maps.co.uk